Stitch Workshop
Peyote Stitch

basic techniques, advanced results

KB
KALMBACH BOOKS

From the publisher of
Bead&Button magazine

Kalmbach Books
21027 Crossroads Circle
Waukesha, Wisconsin 53186
www.Kalmbach.com/Books

Published in 2011
15 14 13 12 11   1 2 3 4 5

Manufactured in the United States of America

ISBN: 978-0-87116-423-0

The material in this book has appeared previously in
Bead&Button magazine and *Brilliant Crystal Jewelry 2*.
Bead&Button is registered as a trademark.

Publisher's Cataloging-in-Publication Data
Peyote stitch : basic techniques, advanced results.

   p. : col. ill. ; cm. -- (Stitch workshop)

   The material in this book has appeared previously in
Bead&Button magazine and Brilliant Crystal Jewelry 2.
   ISBN: 978-0-87116-423-0

   1. Beadwork--Patterns. 2. Beadwork--Handbooks, manuals,
etc. I. Title: Bead & button. II. Title: Brilliant crystal jewelry.
2.

TT860 .P49 2011
745.5942

Contents

Peyote and stitching basics

Projects

Introduction

There are several reasons why peyote stitch is generally acknowledged as the most popular bead stitch. Peyote creates a finely stitched fabric that looks and feels smooth and flexible. It also offers plenty of shaping alternatives and stitch variations, such as tubular and spiral stitches, odd-count, even-count, and two-, three-, and four-drop. And peyote stitch is simple, often the first stitch that new beaders learn.

New beaders and accomplished beaders alike are sure to love this collection of 27 of the best peyote projects featured in *Bead&Button* magazine. Each piece highlights the amazing variety peyote offers: graphed patterns and beaded beads, ruffles and bezels, necklaces, bracelets, pins, and earrings. The projects are organized by level of difficulty, so you can start with a basic peyote band and work your way up to making Cellini spiral and Dutch spiral variants, bezeling stones, weaving layers, and staggering rows. Or jump around, choosing projects that appeal to your personal design aesthetic. Whatever path you take, you'll enjoy the variety of stunning pieces peyote stitch helps you create.

Peyote stitch

While evidence of the technique now known as peyote stitch has been found in various ancient civilizations, the term "peyote stitch" comes from Native American cultures. The beadwork depicted symbols, usually worked around a handle or other object, on artifacts that were used in religious ceremonies. The term "peyote" applied only to beadwork that was used in the Native American Church. When other objects were decorated with the stitch for dancing or nonreligious events, the term "gourd stitch" was given to this beadwork to distinguish it from the religious kind. Over time, all the different styles of this stitch were grouped together and referred to as "peyote stitch." The overall look of peyote stitch is staggered rows of beads. Working off a base row, the basic principle is pick up a bead, skip a bead, and sew through the next bead.

Flat even-count peyote

[1] Pick up an even number of beads (a–b). These beads will shift to form the first two rows.
[2] To begin row 3, pick up a bead, skip the last bead strung in the previous step, and sew through the next bead in the opposite direction (b–c). For each stitch, pick up a bead, skip a bead in the previous row, and sew through the next bead, exiting the first bead strung (c–d). The beads added in this row are higher than the previous rows and are referred to as "up-beads."
[3] For each stitch in subsequent rows, pick up a bead, and sew through the next up-bead in the previous row (d–e). To count peyote stitch rows, count the total number of beads along both straight edges.

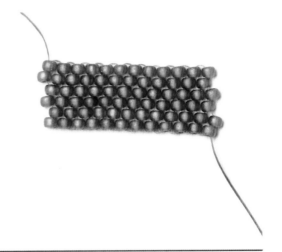

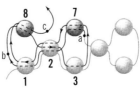

Flat odd-count peyote

Odd-count peyote is the same as even-count peyote, except for the turn on odd-numbered rows, where the last bead of the row can't be attached in the usual way because there is no up-bead to sew through. Work the traditional odd-row turn as follows:
[1] Begin as for flat even-count peyote, but pick up an odd number of beads. Work row 3 as in even-count, stopping before adding the last two beads.
[2] Work a figure-8 turn at the end of row 3: Pick up the next-to-last bead (#7), and sew through #2, then #1 (figure 1, a–b). Pick up the last bead of the row (#8), and sew through #2, #3, #7, #2, #1, and #8 (b–c).

FIGURE 1

[3] You can work this turn at the end of each odd-numbered row, but this edge will be stiffer than the other. Instead, in subsequent odd-numbered rows, pick up the last bead of the row, then sew under the thread bridge immediately below. Sew back through the last bead added to begin the next row.

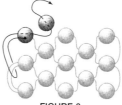

FIGURE 2

[4] Another approach to beginning odd-count peyote eliminates the complicated turn described above, but it requires you to pick up the beads in rows 2 and 3 first:

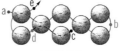

FIGURE 3

Pick up an odd number of beads (figure 3, a–b). These beads will shift to form rows 2 and 3. If you're working a pattern with more than one bead color, make sure you pick up the beads for the correct rows.

[5] To begin the next row (row 1), pick up a bead, skip the last bead strung in the previous step, and sew through the next bead in the opposite direction (b–c). Continue in this manner, exiting the second-to-last bead strung in the previous row (c–d).

[6] For the final stitch in the row, pick up a bead, and sew through the first bead strung (d–e).

[7] To work row 4 and all subsequent even-numbered rows, pick up one bead per stitch, exiting the end up-bead in the previous row (figure 4, a–b). To work row 5 and all

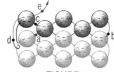

FIGURE 4

subsequent odd-numbered rows, pick up one bead per stitch, exiting the end up-bead in the previous row (b–c). Work a simplified turn as shown (c–d). Sew back through the last bead added to begin the next row (d–e).

Circular peyote

Circular peyote stitch is worked in rounds like tubular peyote (below), but the rounds stay flat and radiate outward from the center as a result of increases. Using larger beads can give the same effect.

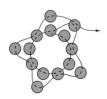 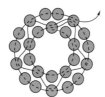 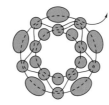

Tubular peyote

Tubular peyote stitch follows the same stitching pattern as flat peyote, but instead of sewing back and forth, you work in rounds to form a tube.

[1] Pick up an even number of beads to equal the desired circumference. Tie a knot to form a ring, leaving some slack.

[2] Put the ring over a form if desired. Sew through the first bead after the knot. Pick up a bead, skip a bead in the previous round, and sew through the next bead. Repeat until you're back at the start.

[3] Since you started with an even number of beads, you need to step up to be in position for the next round. Sew through the first bead added in round 3 (figure 3, a–b). Pick up a bead, and sew through the second bead in round 3 (b–c). Repeat to achieve the desired length.

[4] If you begin with an odd number of beads, you won't need to step up; the beads will automatically form a continuous spiral.

Modified versions of tubular peyote include Dutch spiral and Cellini spiral. In Dutch spiral the twist is created with multiple bead sizes and a loose "bridge" of beads that spans one section of the beadwork. Cellini is worked with beads of varying sizes to create a sculptural look.

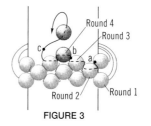

FIGURE 1

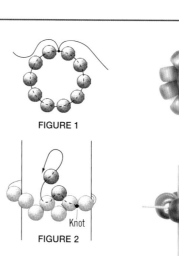

Knot

FIGURE 2

Round 4
Round 3
Round 2   Round 1

FIGURE 3

Decrease

[1] At the point of decrease, go through two beads in the previous row.

[2] In the next row, when you reach the two-bead space, pick up one bead.

Increase

[1] At the point of increase, pick up two beads instead of one. Sew through the next bead.

[2] When you reach the two beads in the next row, sew through the first bead, pick up a bead, and sew through the second bead.

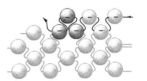

Two-drop peyote

Work two-drop peyote the same as basic flat peyote, but treat pairs of beads as if they were single beads. Start with an even number of beads divisible by four. Pick up two beads (stitch 1 of row 3), skip two beads, and sew through the next two beads. Repeat across the row.

Zipping up or joining

To join two sections of a flat peyote piece invisibly, match up the two pieces so the end rows fit together. "Zip up" the pieces by zigzagging through the up-beads on both ends.

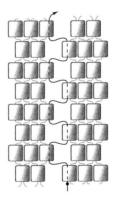

Peyote pattern variations

Create stripes by alternating two colors in the original ring of beads.
• For spiral stripes, pick up a bead of the opposite color as the bead directly below it for each stitch in the round.
• For vertical stripes, pick up a bead of the same color as the bead directly below it for each stitch in the round.
• For horizontal stripes, start with a ring of a single color. Work two or more rounds depending on the desired width of the stripe, and switch to a second color for the next two or more rounds. Alternate colors for the desired length.

Bezels

A single technique can be used for stones of all shapes and sizes, but you may need to adjust the number of beads picked up in the initial ring as well as the number of rounds stitched, depending on the desired results. If you want to make beaded bezels around rivolis or stones that have corners — like square, triangular, and navette shapes — you will need to decrease at the corners.

Round rivoli (16mm)

[1] The figure shows the pattern for making a bezel around a 16mm crystal rivoli. Pick up enough 11º cylinder beads to fit around the circumference of a rivoli or stone, and sew through the first cylinder again to form a ring (round, a–b).
[2] Pick up a cylinder, skip the next cylinder in the ring, and sew through the following cylinder (b–c). Continue working in tubular peyote stitch to complete the round, and step up through the first cylinder added (c–d).
[3] Work the next two rounds in tubular peyote using 15º seed beads (d–e). Keep the tension tight to decrease the size of the ring.
[4] Position the rivoli or stone in the bezel cup. Using the tail thread, work one round of tubular peyote along the other edge using cylinder beads, and two rounds using 15ºs.

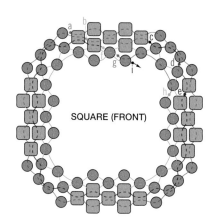

ROUND

Square rivoli (12mm)

[1] On a comfortable length of thread, pick up a repeating pattern of five cylinders and four 15ºs four times, and sew through the first cylinder again (square front, a–b), leaving a 12-in. (30cm) tail.
[2] Work two stitches in tubular peyote using cylinders (b–c). Pick up a 15º, skip the first 15º in the ring, and sew through the next two 15ºs (c–d). Work one stitch with a 15º (d–e). Repeat three times to complete the round, and step up to start the next round (e–f).
[3] Work a round of tubular peyote, picking up one 15º in each stitch, and treating the two 15ºs at each corner as one bead (f–g).
[4] Work a stitch with a 15º, and sew through the next two 15ºs without picking up a new 15º (g–h). Pick up a 15º, and sew through the next up-15º. Continue around, decreasing in the remaining corners the same way (h–i).
[5] Place the rivoli in the bezel, and, using the tail thread, sew through the next 15º in the first round (square back, a–b).
[6] Pick up two 15ºs, sew through the next 15º, and work three peyote stitches using cylinders (b–c). Repeat around, and step up (c–d).
[7] Work a round of tubular peyote using 15ºs, and step up (d–e). Work a second round of 15ºs to complete the bezel, treating the two-bead stitches as a single bead (e–f).

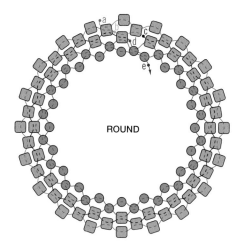

SQUARE (FRONT)

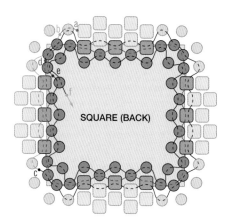

SQUARE (BACK)

Triangular stone (23mm)

[1] On a comfortable length of thread, pick up a repeating pattern of 17 cylinders and five 15ºs three times, leaving an 18-in. (46cm) tail. Sew through the first two cylinders again to form a ring (**triangle, a–b**).

[2] Work seven peyote stitches using cylinders (**b–c**), pick up a 15º, and sew through the next two 15ºs (**c–d**). Pick up a 15º, skip the next 15º in the ring, and sew through the next two 15ºs (**d–e**). Pick up a 15º, skip the next cylinder, and sew through the following cylinder (**e–f**). Repeat around, and step up (**f–g**).

[3] Work a round of tubular peyote, picking up one 15º for each stitch (**g–h**).

[4] Work seven peyote stitches, picking up one 15º in each stitch, and then sew through the next 15º without adding a bead (**h–i**). Continue around in tubular peyote, decreasing in each corner (**i–j**).

[5] Fit the stone in the bezel, and, using the tail thread, pick up two 15ºs, sew through the next 15º, pick up two 15ºs, and sew through the next up-cylinder (**a–aa**). Work eight peyote stitches using cylinders (**aa–bb**). Repeat around the stone, then step up (**bb–cc**).

[6] Work a round of peyote using the same stitch pattern as in step 2: a 15º, a 15º, seven cylinders, a 15º. Repeat around, and step up (**cc–dd**).

[7] Work a round of tubular peyote, picking up one 15º in each stitch, and step up (**dd–ee**).

[8] Work a round of tubular peyote using 15ºs and decreasing in each corner, as in step 4 (**ee–ff**).

Navette stone (32 x 17mm)

[1] On a comfortable length of thread, pick up 29 cylinders and three 15ºs twice, and sew through the first cylinder again to form a ring, leaving an 18-in. (46cm) tail (**navette, a–b**).

[2] Work a round of tubular peyote, picking up cylinders where you skip cylinders and 15ºs where you skip 15ºs (**b–c**).

[3] Work a round of peyote picking up a 15º for each stitch (**c–d**).

[4] Work a round of peyote, picking up one 15º for each stitch on the long sides (where the cylinders sit). Skip the center bead in each corner, picking up two 15ºs to span the distance instead of one (**d–e**).

[5] Place the stone in the bezel so the back is nestled in the beads. If the hold is not secure, you may want to add two 15ºs to each corner.

[6] Using the tail thread, sew through the next 15º (**a–aa**), and work a round of peyote, picking up a 15º in each stitch. Sew through three 15ºs to step up (**aa–bb**).

[7] Work the final round as you did in step 4 (**bb–cc**).

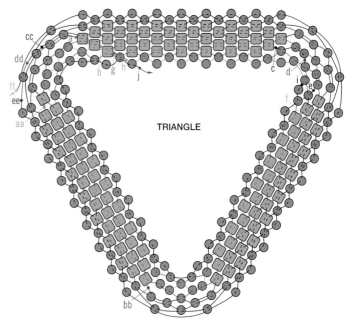

TRIANGLE

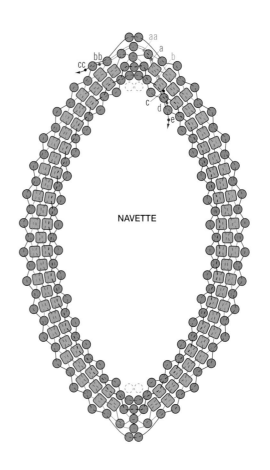

NAVETTE

Basic techniques

Working with thread
Conditioning thread

Use either microcrystalline wax or beeswax (not candle wax or paraffin) or Thread Heaven to condition nylon thread. Wax smooths the nylon fibers and adds tackiness that will stiffen your beadwork slightly. Thread Heaven adds a static charge that causes the thread to repel itself, so don't use it with doubled thread. Stretch the thread, then pull it through the conditioner.

Adding thread

To add a thread, sew into the beadwork several rows prior to the point where the last bead was added. Weave through the beadwork, following the thread path of the stitch. Tie a few half-hitch knots (see **Half-hitch knot**) between beads, and exit where the last stitch ended.

Ending thread

To end a thread, weave back into the beadwork, following the existing thread path and tying two or three half-hitch knots (see **Half-hitch knot**) between beads as you go. Change directions as you weave so the thread crosses itself. Sew through a few beads after the last knot, and trim the thread.

Stop bead

Use a stop bead to secure beads temporarily when you begin stitching. Choose a bead that is distinctly different from the beads in your project. String the stop bead, and sew through it again in the same direction. If desired, sew through it one more time for added security.

Knots
Half-hitch knot

Pass the needle under the thread between two beads. A loop will form as you pull the thread through. Cross back over the thread between the beads, sew through

the loop, and pull gently to draw the knot into the beadwork.

Square knot

[1] Cross the left-hand end of the thread over the right, and bring it under and back up.
[2] Cross the end that is now on the right over the left, go through the loop, and pull both ends to tighten.

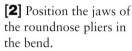

Surgeon's knot

[1] Cross the left-hand end of the thread over the right twice. Pull to tighten.
[2] Cross the end that is now on the right over the left, go through the loop, and tighten.

Wirework
Loops, plain

[1] Using chain-nose pliers, make a right-angle bend approximately ¼ in. (6mm) from the end of the wire.
[2] Grip the tip of the wire with roundnose pliers. Press downward slightly, and rotate the wire into a loop.
[3] Let go, then grip the loop at the same place on the pliers, and keep turning to close the loop. The closer to the tip of the roundnose pliers that you work, the smaller the loop will be.

Loops, wrapped

[1] Using chain-nose pliers, make a right-angle bend approximately 1¼ in. (3.2cm) from the end of the wire.
[2] Position the jaws of the roundnose pliers in the bend.
[3] Curve the short end of the wire over the top jaw of the roundnose pliers.
[4] Reposition the pliers so the lower jaw fits snugly in the loop. Curve the wire downward around the bottom jaw of the pliers. This is the first half of a wrapped loop.
[5] To complete the wraps, grasp the top of the loop with chain-nose pliers.
[6] Wrap the wire around the stem two or three times. Trim the excess wire, and gently press the cut end close to the wraps with chainnose pliers.

Opening and closing plain loops and jump rings

[1] Hold a loop or a jump ring with two pairs of pliers.
[2] To open the loop or jump ring, bring the tips of one pair of pliers toward you, and push the tips of the other pair away from you.
[3] Reverse the steps to close the open loop or jump ring.

Crimping

Use crimp beads to secure flexible beading wire. Slide the crimp bead into place, and squeeze it firmly with chainnose pliers to flatten it. For a more finished look, use crimping pliers:

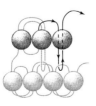

[1] Position the crimp bead in the hole that is closest to the handle of the crimping pliers.

[2] Holding the wires apart, squeeze the pliers to compress the crimp bead, making sure one wire is on each side of the dent.

[3] Place the crimp bead in the front hole of the pliers, and position it so the dent is facing the tips of the pliers. Squeeze the pliers to fold the crimp in half. Tug on the wires to ensure that the crimp is secure.

Stitches
Brick stitch

[1] Begin with a ladder of beads (see **Ladder stitch**), and position the

thread to exit the top of the last bead. The ends of each new row will be offset slightly from the previous row. To work in the typical method, which results in progressively decreasing rows, pick up two beads. Sew under the thread bridge between the second and third beads in the previous row from back to front. Sew up through the second bead added, down through the first bead, and back up through the second bead.

[2] For the row's remaining stitches, pick up one bead per stitch. Sew under the next thread bridge in the previous row

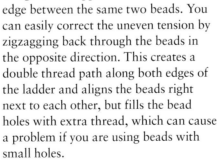

from back to front, and sew back up through the new bead. The last stitch in the row will be positioned above the last two beads in the row below, and the row will be one bead shorter than the previous row.

To increase at the end of the row, add a second stitch to the final thread bridge in the row.

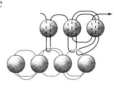

Ladder stitch
Traditional method

[1] Pick up two beads, sew through the first bead again, and then sew through the second bead **(a–b)**.

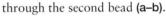

[2] Add subsequent beads by picking up one bead, sewing through the previous bead, and then sewing through the new bead **(b–c)**. Continue for the desired length.

This technique produces uneven tension along the ladder of beads because of the alternating pattern of a single thread bridge on one edge between two beads and a double thread bridge on the opposite edge between the same two beads. You can easily correct the uneven tension by zigzagging back through the beads in the opposite direction. This creates a double thread path along both edges of the ladder and aligns the beads right next to each other, but fills the bead holes with extra thread, which can cause a problem if you are using beads with small holes.

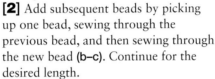

Alternative method

[1] Pick up all the beads you need to reach the length your pattern requires. Fold the last two beads so they are parallel, and sew through the second-to-last bead again in the same direction **(a–b)**.

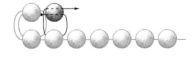

[2] Fold the next loose bead so it sits parallel to the previous bead in the ladder, and sew through the loose bead in the same direction **(a–b)**. Continue sewing back through each bead until you exit the last bead of the ladder.

Square stitch

[1] String the required number of beads for the first row. Then pick up the first bead of the second row. Sew through the last bead of the first row and the first bead of the second row again. The new bead sits on top of the bead in the previous row, and the holes are parallel.

[2] Pick up the second bead of row 2, and sew through the next bead in row 1 and the new bead in row 2. Repeat this step for the entire row.

Tools & materials

Excellent tools and materials for making jewelry are available in bead and craft stores, through catalogs, and on the Internet. Here are the essential supplies you'll need for the projects in this book.

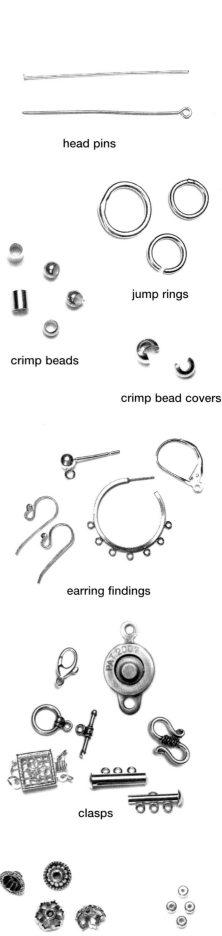

head pins

jump rings

crimp beads

crimp bead covers

earring findings

clasps

bead caps   spacers

Tools

Chainnose pliers have smooth, flat inner jaws, and the tips taper to a point. Use them for gripping and for opening and closing loops and jump rings.

Roundnose pliers have smooth, tapered, conical jaws used to make loops. The closer to the tip you work, the smaller the loop will be.

Use the front of a **wire cutters'** blades to make a pointed cut and the back of the blades to make a flat cut. Do not use your jewelry-grade wire cutters on memory wire, which is extremely hard; use heavy-duty wire cutters or bend the memory wire back and forth until it breaks.

Crimping pliers have two grooves in their jaws that are used to fold or roll a crimp bead into a compact shape.

Beading needles are coded by size. The higher the number, the finer the beading needle. Unlike sewing needles, the eye of a beading needle is almost as narrow as its shaft. In addition to the size of the bead, the number of times you will pass through the bead also affects the needle size that you will use; if you will pass through a bead multiple times, you need to use a smaller needle.

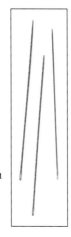

Findings

A **head pin** looks like a long, blunt, thick sewing pin. It has a flat or decorative head on one end to keep beads on. Head pins come in different diameters (or gauges) and lengths.

A **jump ring** is used to connect two loops. It is a small wire circle or oval that is either soldered closed or comes with a split so you can twist the jump ring open and closed.

Crimp beads are small, large-holed, thin-walled metal beads designed to be flattened or crimped into a tight roll. Use them when stringing jewelry on flexible beading wire. **Crimp bead covers** provide a way to hide your crimps by covering them with a finding that mimics the look of a small bead.

Earring findings come in a huge variety of metals and styles, including post, French hook, hoop, and lever-back. You will almost always want a loop (or loops) on earring findings so you can attach beads or beadwork.

Clasps come in many sizes and shapes. Some of the most common are the toggle, consisting of a ring and a bar; lobster claw, which opens when you pull on a tiny lever; S-hook and hook-and-eye, which link two soldered jump rings or split rings; slide, consisting of one tube that slides inside another; snap, consisting of a ball that inserts into a socket; and box, with a tab and a slot.

Bead caps are used to decorate one or both sides of a bead or gemstone.

Spacers are small beads used between larger beads to space the placement of the beads.

Stitching & stringing materials

Thread comes in many sizes and strengths. Size (diameter or thickness) is designated by a letter or number. OO, O, and A are the thinnest threads; B, D, E, F, and FF are subsequently thicker.

Plied gel-spun polyethylene (GSP), such as Power Pro or DandyLine, is made from polyethylene fibers that have been spun into two or more threads that are braided together. It is almost unbreakable, doesn't stretch, and resists fraying. The thickness can make it difficult to make multiple passes through a bead. It is ideal for stitching with larger beads, such as pressed glass and crystals. **Parallel filament GSP**, such as Fireline, is a single-ply thread made from spun and bonded polyethylene fibers. Because it's thin and strong, it's best for stitching with small seed beads.

Other threads are available, including **polyester thread**, such as Gutermann (best for bead crochet or bead embroidery when the thread must match the fabric); **parallel filament nylon**, such as Nymo or C-Lon (best used in bead weaving and bead embroidery); and **plied nylon**

threads

thread, such as Silamide (good for twisted fringe, bead crochet, and beadwork that needs a lot of body).

Flexible beading wire is composed of steel wires twisted together and covered with nylon. This wire is much stronger than thread and does not stretch; the higher the number of inner strands (between three and 49), the more flexible and kink-resistant the wire. It is available in a variety of sizes. Use .014 and .015 for most gemstones, crystals, and glass beads. Use thicker varieties, .018, .019, and .024, for heavy beads or nuggets. Use thinner wire, .010 and .012, for lightweight pieces and beads with very small holes, such as pearls.

flexible beading wire

Memory wire is steel spring wire. It comes in several sizes and can be used without clasps to make coiled bracelets, necklaces, and rings.

memory wire

Beads

Most projects in this book will call for **seed beads** as the main elements of the design. The most common and highest quality seed beads are manufactured in Japan or the Czech Republic. These seed

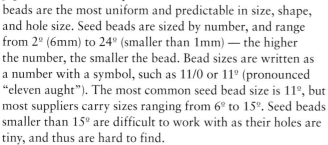

beads are the most uniform and predictable in size, shape, and hole size. Seed beads are sized by number, and range from 2º (6mm) to 24º (smaller than 1mm) — the higher the number, the smaller the bead. Bead sizes are written as a number with a symbol, such as 11/0 or 11º (pronounced "eleven aught"). The most common seed bead size is 11º, but most suppliers carry sizes ranging from 6º to 15º. Seed beads smaller than 15º are difficult to work with as their holes are tiny, and thus are hard to find.

Japanese cylinder beads, which are sold under the brand names Delicas, Treasures, or Aikos, are very consistent in shape and size. Unlike the standard round seed bead, they're shaped like little tubes and have very large, round holes and straight sides. They create an even surface texture when stitched together in beadwork. These beads are also sold in tubes or packages by weight. In addition to round and cylinder beads, there are several other seed bead shapes: **Hex-cut beads** are similar to cylinder beads, but instead of a smooth, round exterior, they

have six sides. **Triangle beads** have three sides, and **cube beads** have four. **Bugle beads** are long, thin tubes that can range in size from 2 to 30mm long. You might also find tiny teardrop-shaped beads, called **drops** or **fringe drops**, and **magatamas**. Cube, drop, and bugle beads are sold by size, measured in millimeters (mm) rather than aught size.

Some projects may also use a variety of **accent beads** to embellish your stitched pieces, including **crystals, gemstones, fire-polished beads**, and **pearls** — to name only a few types.

Electrifying
zigzag stripes

Triangular points create dimensional accents

designed by **Jennifer Creasey**

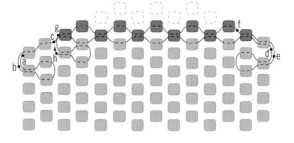

FIGURE 1

FIGURE 2

MATERIALS

bracelet 7 in. (18cm)

- 2 2–3mm accent beads
- 11º Japanese cylinder beads
  3g color A
  3g color B
  2g color C
  2g color D
  2g color E
- clasp
- nylon beading thread, size B or D, conditioned with beeswax or Thread Heaven
- beading needles, #12

Select brightly colored cylinder beads to make the zigzags flash against a darker background. Metallic-finished beads add sparkling highlights.

stepbystep

[1] On 2 yd. (1.8m) of conditioned Nymo, attach a stop bead (Basics, p. 10), leaving a 2-ft. (61cm) tail.

[2] Beginning at the lower left-hand corner of the pattern, pick up 12 color B and two color C Japanese cylinder beads. Stitch the main panel in flat, even-count peyote stitch (Peyote Basics, p. 5).

[3] Taper the ends of the panel as follows: with the thread exiting **figure 1, point a**, turn as shown **(a–b)**. Sew back through the bead at **point a** and the last bead added **(b–c)**. Work six peyote stitches **(c–d)**, turn **(d–e)**, and sew back through the edge bead and the last bead picked up **(e–f)**. Work five peyote stitches **(f–g)**, turn **(g–h)**, and sew back through the edge bead and the last bead picked up. Work two more rows of peyote stitch, decreasing to four beads and then to three beads. Do not trim the tails.

[4] For the points, add 1 yd. (.9m) of Nymo, exiting the edge cylinder indicated by the arrow shown on the pattern.

[5] Picking up the appropriate color cylinders, add the first point in brick stitch (Basics).

[6] Stitch diagonally across the band to the next point on the other side. Continue adding points along the length of the band.

[7] To add the clasp, thread a needle on the tail on one end, turn as you did at the end of each tapered row, and exit at **figure 2, point a**.

[8] Pick up an A, an accent bead, an A, the loop on one clasp half, and an A. Sew back through the accent bead, pick up an A, and sew through the third cylinder on the end row **(a–b)**. Retrace the thread path a few times, and end the thread. Repeat on the other end with the other tail and clasp half.

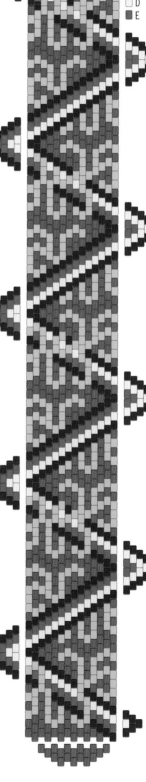

PATTERN

Colorful
connections

Mix and match your favorite colors in this multihued beaded bead bracelet

designed by **Julie Glasser**

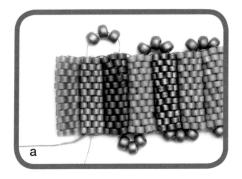

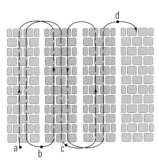

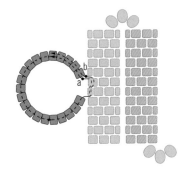

MATERIALS
bracelet 7 in. (18cm)
- 3g size 8º seed beads
- 11º Japanese cylinder beads, 3g in each of **10** colors
- nylon beading thread, size D, conditioned with Thread Heaven
- beading needles, #10

FIGURE 1

FIGURE 2

FIGURE 3

Stack simple tube beads for a textured bracelet

stepbystep

Peyote stitch tube beads

[1] On 2 ft. (61cm) of thread, pick up a stop bead (Basics, p. 10), leaving a 6-in. (15cm) tail. Pick up 12 cylinder beads of a single color, and work 12 rows of flat, even-count peyote stitch (Peyote Basics, p. 5). The completed peyote strip should be 12 cylinders wide, with six cylinders on each straight edge.

[2] Zip up (Peyote Basics) the ends of the strip to form a tube. Remove the stop bead, and end the threads (Basics).

[3] Repeat steps 1 and 2 to make a total of 30 peyote tubes, three in each of 10 colors. Set one aside to use as the toggle bar. To adjust the length of the bracelet, make more or fewer tubes as needed. When lined up side by side, the tubes should be approximately 1/2 in. (1.3cm) short of the desired length.

Assembly

[1] Arrange the tubes side by side as desired.

[2] On 3 yd. (2.7m) of thread, leave a 12-in. (30cm) tail, and pick up two tubes (figure 1, a–b). Working in ladder stitch (Basics), sew through both tubes again (b–c).

[3] Continue joining the remaining tubes (c–d), and exit one end of the last tube.

[4] To make the decorative edge, pick up three 8º seed beads, and sew through the next tube. Repeat, adding 8ºs on alternate edges until you reach the other end of the bracelet (photo a). Tie the working thread to the tail at the beginning of the bracelet using a square knot (Basics).

[5] To attach the toggle bar, use the working thread, and retrace the thread path back through the 8ºs and tubes to the other end of the bracelet.

[6] Zigzag through the cylinders in the end tube to exit the seventh cylinder from one edge (figure 2, point a). Pick up a cylinder, and sew through the sixth cylinder in the tube (a–b). Pick up a cylinder, and sew through the first cylinder added in this step (b–c). Continue working in flat peyote stitch until the toggle strap is at least five cylinders long (c–d).

[7] Sew through two of the middle beads in the tube you set aside for the toggle bar (d–e and photo b). Retrace the thread path several times, and end the working thread.

[8] Thread a needle on the tail, and zigzag through the cylinders in the last tube to exit at figure 3, point a. Pick up 19 to 21 cylinders, and sew through the middle two cylinders again to create a loop (a–b). Pull to tighten, and retrace the thread path several times, and end the thread.

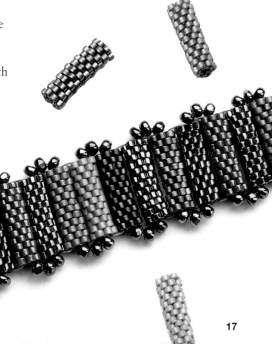

Floral peyote bracelet, fit for a cubist

A rim of cube beads makes flat, circular peyote blossom

designed by **Jean Power**

Early twentieth-century cubists, like Picasso and Cézanne, broke down objects to their simplest forms and often showed multiple angles at once. The cube beads of this bracelet's petals distill the flower design to a basic shape and make the bracelet a blooming beauty, no matter which angle you view it from. Choose an open or solid center as a base, then work the petals. Finish your bracelet with a custom toggle or an integrated clasp.

MATERIALS
bracelet 7¼ in. (18.4cm)
both projects
• 4g 7mm bugle beads
• 7g 4mm cube beads
• 2g size 8º seed beads
• 6g size 11º seed beads
• 1g size 15º seed beads
• nylon beading thread, size D, conditioned with beeswax or Thread Heaven
• beading needles, #12

solid-center bracelet
• 6 4mm fire-polished beads
• 3-strand box clasp

stepbystep

Solid-center bracelet (pink and yellow, opposite)

Center

[1] On 2 yd. (1.8m) of conditioned Nymo (Basics, p. 10), pick up a 4mm fire-polished bead and five 15º seed beads, leaving a 6-in. (15cm) tail. Sew through the 4mm again (figure 1, a–b). Pick up five 15ºs, sew through the 4mm (b–c), and continue around through the first five 15ºs added (c–d).

[2] Pick up two 15ºs, and continue through the next five 15ºs (figure 2, a–b). Pick up two more 15ºs, and sew through the next three 15ºs (b–c).

[3] Using 11º seed beads, work one round in flat, circular peyote stitch (Peyote Basics, p. 5), adding one 11º per stitch and stepping up at the end of the round (figure 3, a–b).

[4] Using 8º seed beads, work one round of flat, circular peyote, stepping up at the end of the round (b–c).

[5] Pick up a 15º, an 8º, and a 15º, and sew through the next 8º (c–d). Repeat around the ring and step up through the first 15º and 8º added in this round (d–e).

Petals

[1] With the thread that is exiting the 8º on the outer rim (figure 4, point a), pick up a bugle bead, an 11º, a cube bead, an 11º, and a bugle. Sew through the 8º and the first bugle again (a–b).

[2] Pick up an 11º, a cube, an 11º, a bugle, and an 11º. Sew through the next 8º in the base (b–c). Pick up an 11º, and sew through the bugle from the previous step and the next four beads, exiting the end bugle (c–d).

[3] To create the petal's shape, skip the base 8º as you sew through both 11ºs (d–e), and tighten. Retrace the thread path to exit at the base of the new bugle, and sew through the next base 8º (e–f).

[4] Pick up a bugle, an 11º, a cube, and an 11º, and sew through the bugle from the previous step, the base 8º, and the new bugle (f–g).

[5] Repeat steps 2–4 until you have 13 cubes along the rim and are exiting a bugle.

[6] To complete the flower, pick up an 11º, a cube, and an 11º. Sew down through the first bugle (figure 5, a–b).

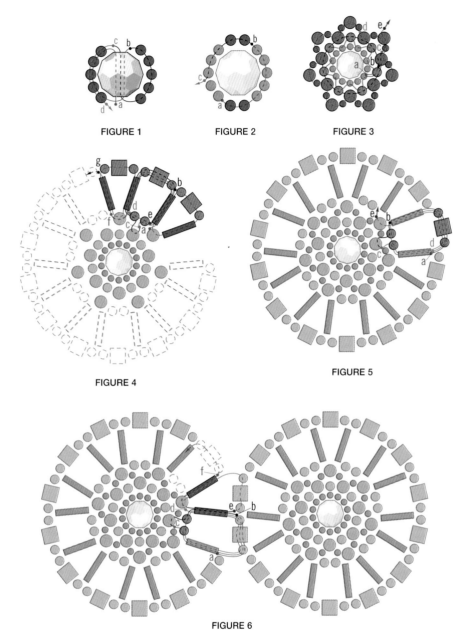

FIGURE 1

FIGURE 2

FIGURE 3

FIGURE 4

FIGURE 5

FIGURE 6

Pick up an 11º, and sew through the adjacent base 8º (b–c). Pick up an 11º, and sew through the last bugle (c–d). Retrace the thread path, skipping the 8º, as in step 3. Exit the next 8º (d–e). End the thread (Basics).

Joining

[1] Make another flower as in steps 1–5 of "Petals," until there are cubes along the rim and you are exiting the outer edge of a bugle.

[2] Instead of picking up new beads for the outer rim, sew through an 11º, a cube, and an 11º from a petal of the previous flower (figure 6, a–b). Pick up a bugle and an 11º, and sew through the base 8º on the incomplete flower (b–c). Pick up an 11º, retrace the thread path, skipping the 8º, and exit the newest bugle (c–d).

[3] Sew through the next base 8º. Pick up a bugle and sew through the 11º, cube, and 11º of the next petal on the previous flower (d–e). Sew through the bugle from step 2 and the base 8º, and exit the newest bugle (e–f).

[4] Finish as in step 6 of the petals, referring to figure 6. Retrace the thread path to reinforce it. End the thread.

[5] Repeat steps 1–4 to complete and join a total of four flowers. The remaining flowers will be adjusted to incorporate the clasp.

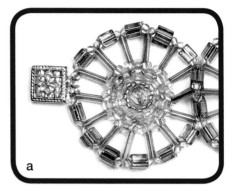

a

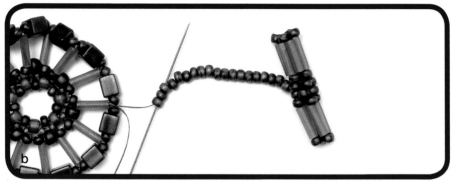

b

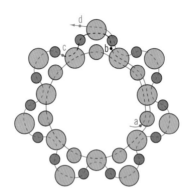

FIGURE 7

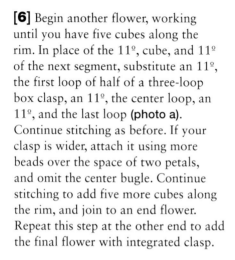

[6] Begin another flower, working until you have five cubes along the rim. In place of the 11º, cube, and 11º of the next segment, substitute an 11º, the first loop of half of a three-loop box clasp, an 11º, the center loop, an 11º, and the last loop **(photo a)**. Continue stitching as before. If your clasp is wider, attach it using more beads over the space of two petals, and omit the center bugle. Continue stitching to add five more cubes along the rim, and join to an end flower. Repeat this step at the other end to add the final flower with integrated clasp.

Open-center bracelet (teal, top right)
[1] On 1 yd. (.9m) of conditioned Nymo, leaving a 10-in. (25cm) tail, pick up an 11º seed bead and an 8º seed bead. Repeat until you have 14 beads. Join the beads into a loose ring by sewing through the first four beads, exiting an 8º **(figure 7, a–b)**.
[2] Pick up a 15º seed bead, an 8º, and a 15º, skip the next 11º, and sew through the following 8º in the ring **(b–c)**. Repeat around the ring, and step up through the first 15º and 8º added in this round **(c–d)**.
[3] Using the 10-in. (25cm) tail, retrace the thread path around the center ring a few times, and end the thread.
[4] Work as in steps 1–6 to complete the first flower.
[5] Work as in steps 1–5 of "Joining" to complete and join a total of six flowers.
[6] On 2 yd. (1.8m) of thread, attach a stop bead (Basics), leaving a 6-in. (15cm) tail. Pick up an 11º, a bugle,

four 11ºs, a bugle, and an 11º. Work a total of eight rows in flat, even-count peyote (Basics) to make a strip that is eight beads wide and has four beads along each flat edge.
[7] Zip up (Peyote Basics) the strip to form a tube. Retrace your thread path through all the rows a few times for added stability. Remove the stop bead, and end the thread.
[8] Add 1 ft. (30cm) of thread in the beadwork, and exit between two petals of one of the end flowers. Pick up 15 to 25 11ºs, sew through a few beads in the center section of 11ºs on the toggle bar, sew back through the 11ºs you added **(photo b)**, and pull tight. Retrace the thread path a few times, secure the tail, and trim.

EDITOR'S NOTE:
To correctly align the bracelet, make sure that five unshared cube sections are between each flower join.

Wave
ring

Whether worn stacked or side by side, these rings make a big splash!

designed by **Cindy Thomas Pankopf**

MATERIALS

one ring (size 8½)

- **8** 3.4mm drop beads
- 1g 8º Japanese seed beads
- 1g 10º Japanese cylinder beads
- 1g 11º Japanese cylinder beads in each of **5** colors: A, B, C, D, E
- Fireline, 6 lb. test
- Thread Heaven
- beading needles, #12 or #13

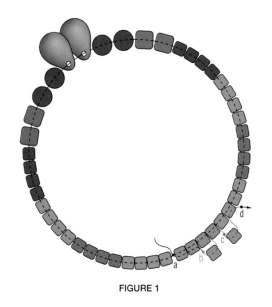

FIGURE 1

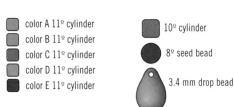

color A 11º cylinder
color B 11º cylinder
color C 11º cylinder
color D 11º cylinder
color E 11º cylinder

10º cylinder
8º seed bead
3.4 mm drop bead

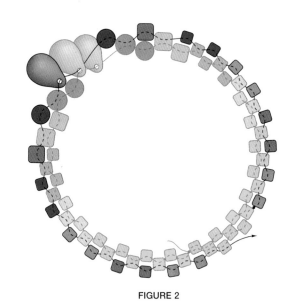

FIGURE 2

Use totally tubular peyote stitch to whip up a handful of beaded rings.

stepbystep

[1] On 1⅓ yd. (1.2m) of conditioned (Basics, p. 10) Fireline, pick up four 11º cylinder beads each of colors A, B, C, D, and E, two 10º cylinder beads, two 8º seed beads, two drop beads, two 8ºs, two 10ºs, four Es, four Ds, four Cs, and four Bs. Tie the beads into a ring with a square knot (Basics), leaving a little slack, and a 12-in. (30 cm) tail. Sew through the first two As (figure 1, a–b).
[2] Working in tubular peyote stitch (Peyote Basics, p. 5), pick up an A, skip an A in the ring, and sew through the next A (b–c). Pick up an A, skip the next B in the ring, and sew through the next B (c–d). To complete the round, continue working in tubular peyote, picking up one bead per stitch in the following

order: B, B, C, C, D, D, E, E, 10º, 8º, drop, 8º, 10º, E, E, D, D, C, C, B, and B. Remember to step up through the first A added in the new round (figure 2).
[3] Continue working in tubular peyote, following the established pattern, to complete a total of eight rounds.
[4] Retrace the last two rounds, and end the working thread (Basics). Repeat with the tail.

Do the twist

Use graduated beads to create a natural twist

by **Anna Elizabeth Draeger**

Hone your spiral peyote skills with this easy bracelet. Use memory wire to hold the tube in the shape of a bracelet, or make the tube longer for a textured, chunky choker.

size 11º seed beads

size 8º seed beads

size 6º seed beads

size 10º triangle beads

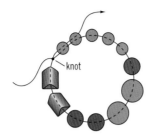

knot

FIGURE 1

FIGURE 2

stepbystep

[1] On a comfortable length of Fireline, pick up five 11º seed beads, one 8º seed bead, two 6º seed beads, two 8ºs, and two 10º triangles. Tie the beads into a ring with a square knot (Basics, p. 10), leaving a 10-in. (25cm) tail. Sew through the first two 11ºs again (figure 1).

[2] Working in tubular peyote stitch (Peyote Basics, p. 5), pick up one bead per stitch in the following order: an 11º, an 11º, an 8º, a 6º, an 8º, and a triangle. Step up through the first 11º added in the round (figure 2).

[3] Repeat step 2 until your tube is 1 in. (2.5cm) shorter than the desired length.

[4] Work three rounds with one 11º per stitch. Work a decrease round with 11ºs:

Pick up an 11º and sew through the next two up-beads. Repeat twice, and step up through the first 11º added in this round. Work one more round with 11ºs. Retrace the thread path of the last round to reinforce it, and pull the beads into a tight ring, and end the thread (Basics).

[5] Cut a piece of memory wire to the length of your tube. With sturdy roundnose pliers, make a small simple loop on each end to prevent the wire ends from poking out of the beadwork. Insert the memory wire into the tube. If the bracelet doesn't hold its shape, insert a second piece of memory wire.

[6] Using the tail, repeat step 4 on the other end of the bracelet.

MATERIALS
bracelet 10 in. (25cm)
- 5–10g 6º seed beads
- 5–10g 8º seed beads
- 5–10g 10º triangle beads
- 5–10g 11º seed beads
- Fireline, 6 lb. test
- beading needles, #10
- memory wire, bracelet diameter
- heavy duty wire cutters
- roundnose pliers

DESIGNER'S NOTE:
To make a necklace, simply make a longer tube, and insert a length of necklace-diameter memory wire into the tube.

Lively links

Connect ruffled rings to create an organic-looking chain

designed by **Marina Nadke**

a

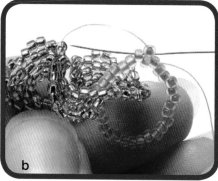

b

c

MATERIALS

necklace 17 in. (43cm)
- 6–8g 11º seed beads in each of 7 colors: A, B, C, D, E, F, G
- 4mm snap fastener
- nylon beading thread, size D
- beading needles, #12

Ready to take a step beyond a chain of peyote links? Ruffle the links for an entirely new dimension of texture.

step by step

Ruffled rings

[1] On 1 yd. (.9m) of thread, pick up 30 color A 11º seed beads, and tie them into a ring with a square knot (Basics, p. 10), leaving a 1-in. (2.5cm) tail. Sew through the ring again, pulling the knot to hide it in the beadwork. Trim the tail.

[2] Work one round of tubular peyote stitch and step up through the first A added in the new round **(figure 1)** (Peyote Basics, p. 5).

[3] Pick up two As, and sew through the next A in the previous round **(figure 2, a–b)**. Continue working a round of two-drop peyote stitch (Peyote Basics), sewing through one up-bead and adding

two As per stitch, and step up through the first two As **(b–c)**.

[4] Work two more rounds of two-drop peyote stitch, sewing through two up-beads and adding two As per stitch, and step up **(figure 3)**. End the thread (Basics).

[5] On 1 yd. (.9m) of thread, pick up 30 color B 11º seed beads. Slide them through the previous ruffled ring, and use a square knot to tie them into a ring **(photo a)**. Sew through the new ring again, pulling the knot to hide it in the beadwork, and trim the tail. Work a round of tubular peyote stitch as in step 2 **(photo b)**, turning the beadwork as you go. Repeat steps 3–4, turning the work as you go.

[6] Attach 32 more ruffled rings, as in step 5, cycling through the 11º seed

FIGURE 1

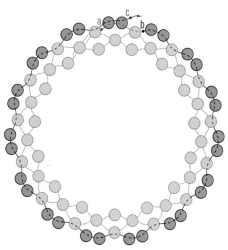

FIGURE 2

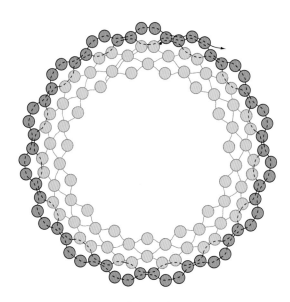

FIGURE 3

The secret clasp snaps through the end links to create a ruffle with a hidden closure.

bead colors and ending with color F 11º seed beads.

Clasp

[1] On 1 yd. (.9m) of thread, attach a stop bead (Basics), leaving a 10-in. (25cm) tail. Pick up 38 color G 11º seed beads, and work a row of flat even-count peyote (Basics and **figure 4, a–b**).
[2] To turn, work a stitch (**b–c**), then work a row of two-drop peyote stitch, sewing through one up-bead and adding two Gs per stitch (**c–d**).
[3] To turn, work a stitch, then work a row of two-drop peyote stitch, sewing through two Gs and adding two Gs per stitch (**d–e**). Repeat (**e–f**).

[4] Sew through the beadwork to exit between two Gs near the end of the strip, and pick up half of the snap (**photo c**). Sew through an adjacent bead in the beadwork. Retrace the thread path a couple of times to reinforce the connection, sewing through all of the open holes of the snap. End the thread.
[5] Remove the stop bead, and thread a needle on the tail. Repeat step 4 with the other half of the snap.

FIGURE 4

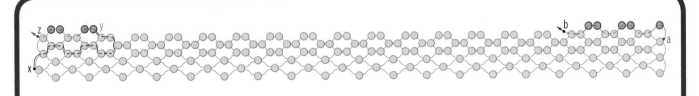

EDITOR'S NOTES
• To make a bracelet, make enough links to reach your desired length.
• If your snap is slightly wider than the beadwork, you can work a partial row to hide it. Work a turn and two two-drop stitches on the working end

(figure, a–b), and end the thread. Remove the stop bead on the opposite end, and sew through the beadwork to exit two two-drop stitches from the end (x–y). Work two two-drop stitches (y–z), and end the tail.

Ruffles & ridges

Stitch a peyote tube bracelet with jaunty twists

designed by **Beth Stone**

Rows of peyote increases produce graceful, rippled edges along tube-shaped beaded beads. Make five, then string them with interesting accent beads to create a lively bracelet. There are no limits to the color combinations you can try for these beads, and feel free to substitute beads in other styles and sizes for the 11ºs.

stepbystep

Ruffled bead
[1] Condition 2 yd. (1.8m) of beading thread (Basics, p. 10), and center eight color A 11º seed beads. Using As, work in flat, even-count peyote (Peyote Basics, p. 5) for 10 rows.
[2] Roll the beadwork into a tube, and zip it up (Peyote Basics) to form a tube. Sew through the beadwork so your needle exits the opposite end from the tail.
[3] Pick up three color B 11º seed beads, and sew under the first thread bridge along the tube's edge and back through the last bead to form a picot **(figure 1, a–b)**.
[4] Pick up two Bs, sew under the next thread bridge, and sew back through the last bead added **(b–c)**.
[5] Repeat step 4 twice **(c–d)**.
[6] Pick up one B **(d–e)** and sew down through the first B in the round, under the corresponding thread bridge, and back through the first two Bs in the round **(e–f)**.
[7] Pick up two As and sew through the next center B in the picot row **(figure 2, a–b)**. Repeat around the tube four more times, picking up a total of ten Bs **(b–c)**. Step up through the first A in the new round **(figure 3, a–b)**.
[8] Pick up one B, and sew through the next A **(b–c)**. Repeat nine times, picking up a total of ten Bs **(c–d)**. Step up through the first B in the new round **(figure 4, a–b)**.
[9] Pick up two As in every stitch in the round for a total of 20 As **(b–c)**. Step up through the first A in the new round.
[10] Repeat step 8 **(figure 5, a–b)**, picking up a total of 20 Bs **(b–c)**. End the thread.
[11] Repeat steps 3–10 on the other edge of the tube.

[12] Repeat steps 1–11 to make a total of five beads, using additional colors as desired.

Toggle ring
[1] On 1 yd. (.9m) of thread, pick up 26 As, leaving a 6 in. (15cm) tail. Using Bs, work a row of peyote **(figure 6, a–b)**.
[2] Picking up two As per stitch, work an increase row **(b–c)**. Repeat to stitch another increase row with As **(c–d)**. Repeat again with Bs **(d–e)**.
[3] Curve the strip to form a twisted oval, and sew the short ends together.

Assembly
[1] String a 10mm bead on a head pin, and make a wrapped loop (Basics).
[2] On 12 in. (30cm) of beading wire, string a crimp bead and two Bs. Go through two outside Bs on the toggle ring, string two Bs, and go back through the crimp bead. Crimp the crimp bead (Basics) and trim the excess wire.

MATERIALS
bracelet 8 in. (20cm)
- 5 8–12mm accent beads, various shapes, colors, and sizes
- 2g 11º Japanese seed beads, in each of **2** colors per beaded bead: A, B
- 10–30 4–6mm spacer beads, various sizes
- 10mm bead for clasp
- beading thread, size D, conditioned with beeswax
- beading needles, #12
- 2-in. (5cm) head pin
- 12 in. (30cm) flexible beading wire, .014
- 2 crimp beads
- chainnose pliers
- crimping pliers
- roundnose pliers
- wire cutters

[3] String 6½ in. (16cm) of spacers, ruffled tubes, and accent beads as desired, then string a crimp bead and the wrapped loop from step 1.
[4] Go back through the crimp and the next few beads. Snug up the beads, crimp the crimp bead, and trim the excess wire.

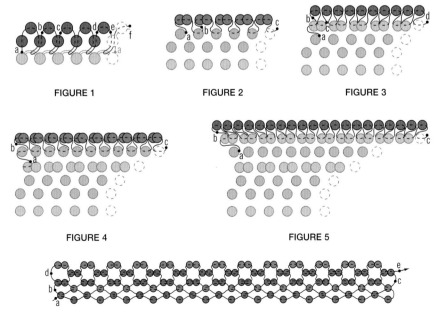

FIGURE 1

FIGURE 2

FIGURE 3

FIGURE 4

FIGURE 5

FIGURE 6

Dimensional
diamonds

Stitch diamond shapes into a peyote pattern to create a textured cuff

designed by **Angie Weathers**

MATERIALS
cuff 8 in. (20cm) circumference
- 5g 11º seed beads
- 10g 11º Japanese cylinder beads
- 4g 15º seed beads
- Fireline, 6 lb. test
- beading needles, #12

Combining different types and sizes of seed beads in a peyote stitch cuff can add interest to a flat band. Carefully placed increases and decreases make creating this geometric design an easy way to familiarize yourself with this technique.

stepbystep

Maintain even tension as you work. If your stitches are too tight, your diamond sections will pucker, and if your stitches are too loose, the thread will show. Work with comfortable lengths of Fireline, ending and adding thread (Basics, p. 10) as needed. Refer to **figure 1** as you stitch.

[1] Pick up 23 11º Japanese cylinder beads, leaving a 10-in. (25cm) tail. Work in odd-count peyote stitch (Peyote Basics, p. 5) for a total of 15 rows of cylinders.

[2] To work a diamond section, pick up one bead per stitch, as follows:

Row 16: Five cylinders, one 11º seed bead, and five cylinders.

Row 17: Five cylinders, two 11ºs, and five cylinders.

Row 18: Four cylinders, three 11ºs, and four cylinders.

Row 19: Four cylinders, four 11ºs, and four cylinders.

Row 20: Three cylinders, five 11ºs, and three cylinders.

Row 21: Three cylinders, six 11ºs, and three cylinders.

Row 22: Two cylinders, seven 11ºs, and two cylinders.

Rows 23–28: Work rows 16–21 in reverse.

[3] Repeat rows 1–28 until you have a total of nine diamond sections.

[4] To create the cuff, zip up (Peyote Basics) the first and last row **(figure 2)**, and sew through the beadwork to exit a cylinder along one edge of the cuff **(figure 3, point a)**.

[5] To make the edge embellishment, pick up four 15º seed beads, and align the beads along the edge of the cuff. Sew through the cylinder closest to the last 15º picked up **(a–b)**. Sew through the previous cylinder along the edge, and the last two 15ºs **(b–c)**. Repeat, adding edging around the cuff. Repeat on the other edge, and end the working thread and tail.

EDITOR'S NOTE:
Always looking for ways to make a project in half the time and with half the materials? Try making a cuff with 10º cylinders in place of 11º cylinders, 8º seed beads in place of 11º seed beads, and 11º cylinders in place of 15º seed beads. Start with 11 10º cylinders for the first row.

DESIGNER'S NOTE:
If you would rather work in even-count peyote, start with 22 cylinders, omitting one cylinder along the edge of the pattern. Then work a row of brick stitch (Basics) along the same edge to center the diamonds.

FIGURE 1

FIGURE 2

FIGURE 3

In full bloom

Crystals accentuate flowers in a peyote bracelet

designed by **Jennifer Creasey**

Jennifer is passionate about patterns — and peyote stitch is a pattern lover's dream! Peyote can give you a finished piece that looks intricate but works up quickly. In this project, crystals connect bands with a repeating floral pattern in a bracelet that's deceptively simple.

MATERIALS
bracelet 7 in. (18cm)
- **16** 6mm bicone crystals
- **2** 4mm bicone crystals
- Japanese cylinder beads
    6g black, color A
    3g dark pink, color B
    3g green, color C
    1g yellow, color D
    1g purple, color E
    1g orange, color F
- nylon beading thread, size D, conditioned with beeswax or Thread Heaven
- beading needles, #12

stepbystep

Toggle bar

[1] On 1 yd. (.9m) of conditioned thread (Basics, p. 10), attach a stop bead (Basics), leaving a 6-in. (15cm) tail. Pick up 10 color A cylinder beads, and work in flat, even-count peyote (Peyote Basics, p. 5) for a total of 12 rows.

[2] Remove the stop bead, and zip up (Basics) the end rows to form a tube **(photo a)**.

[3] Sew through a few rows on the tube to stiffen it. Position the thread so it exits the middle of the peyote tube instead of an edge bead.

[4] Pick up a 4mm bicone crystal and an A. Sew back through the crystal and the peyote tube **(photo b)**.

[5] Repeat step 4 at the other end of the tube, and end the thread.

Peyote band

[1] With 2 yd. (1.8m) of conditioned thread, leave an 8-in. (20cm) tail and start at **point a** on the pattern. Work part 1 in flat, even-count peyote. Decrease (Basics) as needed.

[2] Sew through the beadwork and exit at **point b**. Continue in flat, even-count peyote to work part 2 of the pattern.

[3] Turn the pattern, start a new thread, and work part 3 as you did part 1.

[4] Align the last row of part 2 and the first row of part 3, and zip them together, sewing through the up-beads.

[5] Position your needle so it exits at **point c**, and work part 4 of the pattern. Zip the last row of part 4 to the first row of part 1.

Clasp assembly

[1] Thread a needle on the tail, and sew through to the single bead on the end row **(point d)**. Pick up three As, sew through a bead at the center of the toggle bar, and pick up three As. Sew through the center bead on the end of

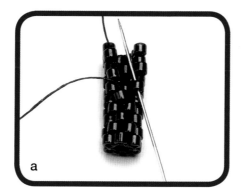

a

b

the band to attach the toggle with a loop of beads. Retrace the thread path a few times, and end the thread.

[2] Add a thread at the other end of the band, and exit the single bead on the end row. Pick up 24 As, and sew through the center end bead again. Adjust the number of beads in the loop as necessary so it fits around the toggle bar. Retrace the thread path a few times, and end the thread.

Crystal accents

[1] Add a new thread in the beadwork, and exit the bead at **point e**.

[2] Pick up an A, a 6mm crystal, and an A. Sew through the bead at **point f**.

[3] Sew through the beadwork and exit at **point g**. Pick up an A, a 6mm crystal, and an A. Sew through the bead at **point h**.

[4] Continue adding crystals along the center of the band as indicated by the arrows on the pattern. End the threads.

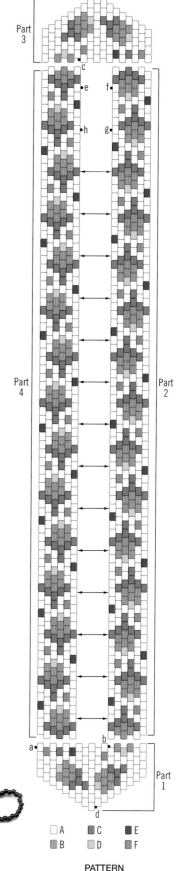

Part 3

Part 4

Part 2

Part 1

☐ A	■ C	■ E
■ B	☐ D	■ F

PATTERN

Bead around the bend

Work tubular peyote stitch around curvy drinking straws to create a lightweight necklace with pizzazz

designed by **Linda Gettings**

You can enclose almost anything in peyote stitch, but these durable drinking straws work particularly well because you can string right through their hollow cores. Worked in bold colors, the sinuous curves make a striking conversation piece.

stepbystep

Peyote stitch straws

[1] Cut two straws to the desired length (photo a). File the rough edges before you begin stitching.

[2] On 2 yd. (1.8m) of thread or Fireline, leave a 6-in. (15cm) tail, and pick up enough 11º seed or cylinder beads to fit around a straw. Tie the beads into a ring with a square knot (Basics, p. 10), and sew through the next bead.

[3] Holding the ring of beads in place on the straw, work in tubular peyote stitch (Peyote Basics, p. 5) in your chosen colors. To make thick bands of color, as in the orange necklace at left, work three to seven rows per color in a random pattern. To make a color gradation, as in the blue necklace, p. 36, work two rows of each color from dark to light, and then work the colors in reverse. Add thread (Basics) as needed. To keep the beadwork smooth, you'll need to decrease along the inside edge of the curves by stitching through previous rows for a few rounds until the beadwork on the outside edge of the curve catches up to the inside edge.

[4] Cinch each end of the peyote tube around the straw

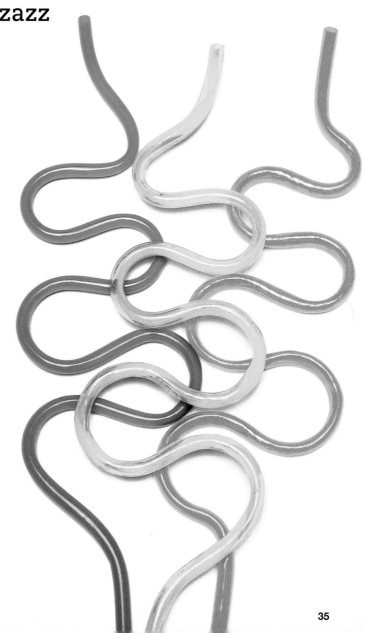

by sewing through the beads of the end row (photo b). End the thread (Basics).

[5] Repeat steps 2–4 with the second straw.

Assembly, necklace with clasp (orange necklace)

[1] Lay out the beads you will use for the neck strap and any others you want to string between the straws and the pendant.

[2] To determine what length of beading wire to cut, temporarily string a beaded straw onto the beading wire. Grasp the beading wire where it exits the straw, remove the straw, and measure the wire. Double that amount, add the length of the remaining beads, and add 6 in. (15cm).

Cut a piece of beading wire to that length. This 22-in. (56cm) necklace required approximately 1 yd. (.9m) of beading wire.

[3] Center the pendant between two 4mm beads (photo c).

[4] Over both wire ends, string three to five accent beads (photo d).

[5] Separate the wire ends, and on each end, string a 4mm, a 6mm bead, a 4mm, and a peyote-covered straw (photo e).

[6] On each end, string 4½ in. (11.4cm) of assorted

accent beads, a crimp bead, a 6º, and one half of the clasp. Go back through the last three or four beads strung (photo f), crimp the crimp bead (Basics), and trim the excess wire.

Assembly, over-the-head necklace (blue necklace)

[1] Follow steps 1 and 2 of the orange necklace. This 32-in. (81cm) necklace required approximately 4½ ft. (1.4m) of beading wire.

[2] On a head pin, string a focal bead and accent beads

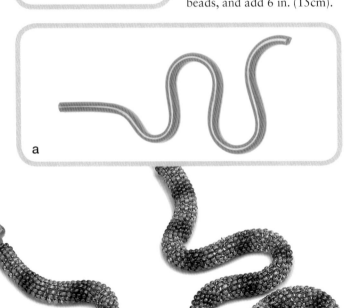

a

b

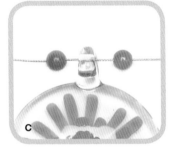

c

d

MATERIALS
necklace 22–32 in. (56–81cm)

- focal bead or pendant
- assorted 4–20mm accent beads and spacers
- 1–2g size 6º seed beads
- 5g size 11º seed or cylinder beads, in each of **5–7** colors
- clasp (optional)
- 3-in. (7.6cm) head pin (optional)
- **2** crimp beads
- nylon beading thread, size D, or Fireline, 6 lb. test
- flexible beading wire, .018 with 7 internal strands
- beading needles, #12
- **1–2** curvy drinking straws
- metal file or coarse nail file
- T-pin (optional)
- chainnose pliers (optional)
- crimping pliers
- roundnose pliers (optional)
- wire cutters

as desired, and make a plain or wrapped loop (Basics) above the beads (photo g).

[3] Center the loop on the beading wire. Over both wire ends, string beads as desired (photo h).

[4] Separate the wires, and, on each end, string two to four accent beads or spacers and a peyote-covered straw (photo i).

[5] On each end, string approximately 4 in. (10cm) of accent beads, a crimp bead, 1–2 in. (2.5–5cm) of accent beads, and 2–3 in. (5–7.6cm) of 6ºs (photo j).

[6] With one wire end, go through the beads on the other end in reverse until you get one or two beads past the crimp bead (photo k). Repeat with the other end, going in the opposite direction. Snug up the beads, crimp the crimp beads, and trim the excess wire.

Margaret Zinser made the focal bead shown here. To see more of her beads, visit her website, mzglass.com.

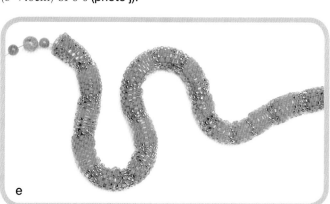

e

f

EDITOR'S NOTE:
To make a necklace with a centered peyote stitch component, as in the teal necklace (above, right), work peyote stitch around a short section of straw. Use a T-pin to pierce the bottom edge at the center of the straw. Center your focal beads on the beading wire, pass both wire ends through the hole you made in the straw, and guide one wire end out through each side of the straw.

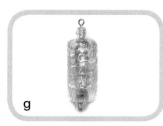

g

h

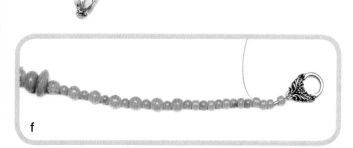

i

j

k

Holler for hoops

Perfect your peyote skills with these quick-to-stitch earrings

designed by **Jonna Holston**

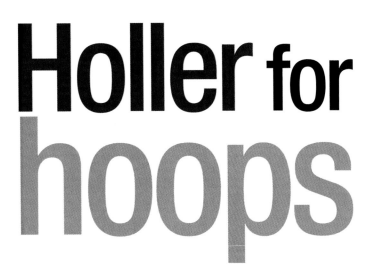

My favorite challenge is to take an object in a different medium — metal, pottery, fabric, or glass — and translate it into a beaded piece of jewelry. An off-center metal circle component on a necklace inspired these earrings.

stepbystep

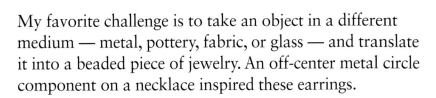

[1] On 1½ yd. (1.4m) of Fireline, pick up an 11º seed bead, an 8º seed bead, an 11º, and 25 15º seed beads, leaving a 6-in. (15 cm) tail. Sew through the first four beads again to form a ring **(photo a)**.

[2] Working in circular peyote stitch (Peyote Basics, p. 5), pick up a 15º, skip a 15º, and sew through the next 15º. Repeat 11 times around, and end by sewing through the 11º, 8º, 11º, the first 15º in the previous round, and the first 15º picked up in this step **(photo b)**.

[3] In rows 3–8, you will decrease each row by one bead. To avoid sewing through the top three beads as each new row is added, reverse the stitching direction by making a turn at the end of each row.

Row 3: Work 11 peyote stitches using cylinder beads. Reverse direction by exiting the last 15º in the previous round, sewing through the 15º directly below it, and sewing back through the last cylinder added in this row **(photo c)**.

Row 4: Work 10 peyote stitches using cylinders. Reverse direction by exiting the last cylinder in row 3, sewing through the 15º directly below it, and sewing back through the last cylinder added in this row.

Row 5: Work nine peyote stitches using hex-cut beads **(photo d)**. Reverse direction by exiting the last cylinder in row 4, sewing through the 15º directly below it, and sewing back through the last hex-cut added in this row.

Row 6: Work eight peyote stitches using hex-cuts. Reverse direction by exiting the last hex-cut in row 5, sewing through the cylinder directly below it, and sewing back through the last hex-cut added in this row.

Row 7: Work seven peyote stitches using triangle beads **(photo e)**. Reverse direction by exiting the last hex-cut in row 6, sewing through the cylinder directly below it, and sewing back through the last triangle added in this row.

a

b

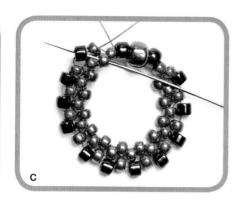

c

d

e

f

g

h

i

Row 8: Work six peyote stitches using triangles. Do not make the turn as described in previous rows.

[4] In rows 9–12, you will increase each row by one bead by beginning the row with an even-count peyote stitch, and ending the row sewing through the same type of bead from a previous row.

Row 9: Work seven peyote stitches using hex-cuts. After adding the last hex-cut, sew through the last hex-cut in row 6, and the next hex-cuts, two cylinders, two 15ºs, the 11º, the 8º, the 11º, two 15ºs, two cylinders, and a hex-cut **(photo f)**.

Row 10: Work eight peyote stitches using hex-cuts. Snug up the beads to form a three-dimensional arch **(photos g and h)**.

Row 11: Work nine peyote stitches using cylinders. Snug up the beads.

Row 12: Work 10 peyote stitches using cylinders. Sew through the next cylinder, two 15ºs, the 11º, the 8º, the 11º, and two 15ºs.

[5] Work 11 peyote stitches using 15ºs. Sew through the top six beads and the next two 15ºs.

[6] Zip up (Basics) the first and last rows of 15ºs.

[7] Sew through a 15º, an 11º, and the 8º. Pick up two 15ºs, an earring finding, and two 15ºs, and sew through the 8º again **(photo i)**. Snug up the beads. Retrace the thread path a few times. Alternatively, you may choose to string ¼ in. (6mm) of French (bullion) wire between two pairs of 15ºs. Secure the working thread and tail, and trim.

[8] Make a second earring.

MATERIALS
pair of earrings
- seed beads
  2 size 8º
  4 size 11º
  104 size 15º
- **80** size 11º cylinder beads
- **64** size 11º hex-cut beads
- **26** size 11º triangle beads
- pair of earring findings
- French (bullion) wire (optional)
- Fireline, 4 lb. test
- beading needles, #13

Take it easy

Loops of beads cross over a two-drop peyote band for a luxurious bracelet

designed by **Karmen Schmidt**

Embellishing a basic stitched band is a classic beading technique that can result in a lush and impressive bracelet. Depending upon the approach, however, it can be a time-consuming undertaking. By using loops of beads, you can add a rich fullness to beaded projects without a lot of fuss.

stepbystep

Two-drop peyote base

[1] Thread a needle with 2 yd. (1.8m) of conditioned thread (Basics, p. 10), and pick up a stop bead (Basics), leaving a 6-in. (15cm) tail.

[2] Pick up 18 cylinder beads (figure 1, a–b). Then pick up two cylinders, skip the last two, and go through the next two (b–c). Pick up two cylinders in each of the next three two-drop peyote (Peyote Basics, p. 5) stitches (c–d).

[3] To secure the last stitch on this row, turn as in odd-count peyote (Peyote Basics): Go through the first two beads in row 1 (d–e). Pick up two cylinders, then go diagonally through the last stitch of row 2 and the second-to-last stitch of row 1 (e–f). Turn, and go diagonally through the second-to-last stitch of row 3 and the last on rows 2 and 1 (f–g). Go back through the two beads just added (g–h).

[4] Make four stitches to complete row 4 as shown in **figure 2**.

[5] For row 5, pick up two beads per stitch across the row (figure 3, a–b). Go under the thread bridge between the

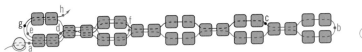

FIGURE 1

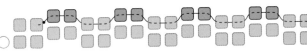

FIGURE 2

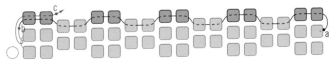

FIGURE 3

two rows below, and go back through the last two beads added in the opposite direction (b–c).

[6] Continue stitching in two-drop peyote until your band is about as long as the circumference of your wrist. Add new thread as needed.

[7] To make the flaps that will attach the band to the clasp, decrease by one stitch on each side of the band. Begin by exiting at figure 4, point a. Go under the thread bridge below, and go back through the two beads you just exited (a–b).

[8] Make three stitches to complete the first row (b–c).

[9] Turn, and make four stitches to complete the second row of the flap. Sew under the thread bridge below (c–d) and back through the last two beads added.

[10] Continue in two-drop peyote for six more rows (d–e). Do not finish off the tail yet.

[11] Repeat steps 7–10 on the other end of the band.

Loops

[1] Center a needle on 4 yd. (3.7m) thread, and, working with the thread doubled, secure it in the beadwork near one end of the band (not the flaps). Sew through the beadwork to exit the second bead from the edge in the first row (figure 5, point a).

[2] Pick up four color A 11º seed beads, a color B 11º, a color C 11º, a color D 11º, a 4mm crystal, a D, a C, a B, and four As. Cross the beads over the band, and sew through the second bead from the other edge (a–b).

[3] Pick up the same bead sequence, cross the beads over the band, and sew through the second bead from the edge in the next row (b–c). Repeat (c–d) for the length of the band.

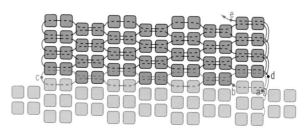

FIGURE 4

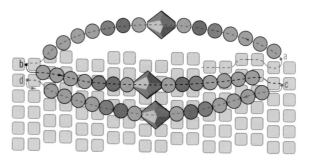

FIGURE 5

Clasp

[1] Slide one of the clasp bars onto a flap, and wrap the flap around the bar.

[2] Thread a needle on the tail from the flap, and stitch the flap to the underside of the first row of the band (photo a). Retrace the thread path for strength. Secure the tail in the beadwork with half-hitch knots (Basics), dot them with glue, and trim.

[3] Making sure the band is not twisted and the clasp is properly oriented, repeat on the other end with the other clasp bar.

a

MATERIALS
bracelet 7 in. (18cm)
- **200** (approximately) 4mm bicone crystals or fire-polished beads
- 10g Japanese cylinder beads
- size 11 seed beads
  20g color A
  5g in each of **3** complementary colors: B, C, D
- tube-style clasp with 21mm side bar
- nylon beading thread, size B or D
- beading needles, #11 or #12
- beeswax or Thread Heaven
- G-S Hypo Cement (optional)

EDITOR'S NOTE:

If you can't find a clasp with a bar end, use a clasp with four loops instead. Stitch the band as indicated, but omit the flaps. Exit one end of the band between the two up-beads in the first column (photo b). Pick up four or five cylinder beads, and an end loop on the clasp, and sew back into the band in the same place (photo c). Retrace the thread path a few times for security, then sew through the beadwork to exit between the next two up-beads. Repeat to attach each loop to the band.

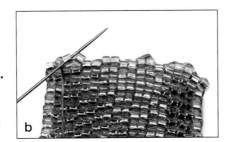

b

c

Capture a refined cuff

A platform of two-drop peyote peeks through open netting sprinkled with lustrous pearls or glittering crystals

designed by **Barbara Klann**

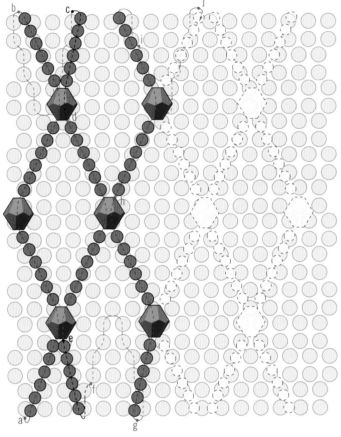

FIGURE 1

For all its glamour, this bracelet is less complicated than it looks. Once you've finished your peyote base, the netting and edges stitch up quickly. Monochromatic palettes lend sophistication, or you can highlight your accent beads with contrasting netting. Sew on a few snaps for a bracelet of uninterrupted style that's sure to catch plenty of attention.

stepbystep

Base
[1] On 2 yd. (1.8m) of conditioned thread (Basics, p. 10), pick up a stop bead (Basics), leaving a 6-in. (15cm) tail. Pick up 24 color A 11º seed beads, then work in flat, two-drop peyote stitch (Peyote Basics, p. 5) using A 11ºs until your band is 24 beads wide and the desired length. Add and end thread (Basics) as needed. Make sure that the number of rows is divisible by 3.
[2] Remove the stop beads, and end the threads.

Netting
Maintain consistent tension while stitching the netting, but don't pull too tightly, or the base may curl.
[1] Add 2 yd. (1.8m) of conditioned thread in the beadwork, exiting an end bead stack on one edge of the cuff **(figure 1, point a)**.
[2] Pick up six 15ºs, a 4mm crystal or pearl, six 15ºs, a 4mm, six 15ºs, a 4mm, and six 15ºs **(a–b)**. Sew through the end bead stack on the opposite edge of the bracelet, and sew through the base, skipping two bead stacks, to exit the fourth bead stack on the same edge **(b–c)**.
[3] Pick up six 15ºs and sew back through the last 4mm added in the

a

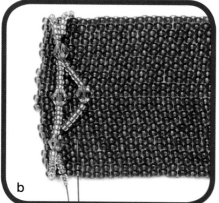

b

EDITOR'S NOTE:
If you've made your bracelet shorter (6½–7 in./16.5–18cm), instead of overlapping with snaps, attach a purchased clasp with reinforced loops of seed beads.

c

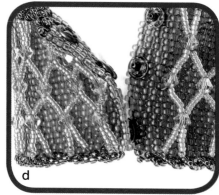

d

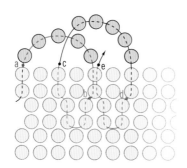

FIGURE 2

previous step (c–d and **photo a**). Pick up six 15ºs, a 4mm, and six 15ºs, and sew through the first 4mm added in the previous step (d–e). Pick up six 15ºs and sew through the fourth bead stack on the opposite edge (e–f and **photo b**). Sew through the base to exit the seventh bead stack along the same edge (f–g).

[4] Pick up six 15ºs, a 4mm, and six 15ºs, and sew through the center 4mm added in the previous step (g–h). Pick up six 15ºs, a 4mm, and six 15ºs, and sew through the seventh bead stack along the opposite edge (h–i). Sew through the base, and exit the tenth bead stack along the same edge (i–j).

[5] Repeat steps 3 and 4, skipping two bead stacks with each horizontal movement, until you're ¼ in. (6mm) from the end, allowing room for the overlap of the snaps.

[6] Secure each end's center 4mm to the base with a few thread paths to maintain the netted spacing (**photo c**). End the thread.

Edging

[1] Add 2 yd. (1.8m) of thread in the base, and exit an end bead stack along one edge (**figure 2, point a**).

[2] Pick up five color B 11ºs, skip three bead stacks, and sew through the base as shown (a–b).

[3] Gently tighten the loop. Sew through the beadwork to exit at **point c**. Make sure to always exit in front of the loop you've just made.

[4] Pick up five Bs, skip three bead stacks, and sew through the base (entering the seventh bead stack), gently tightening the loop (c–d).

[5] Sew back through the base to begin another loop (d–e), and continue in this manner until you reach the end of the base. End the threads.

[6] Repeat steps 1–5 along the other edge.

Clasp

Add 1 yd. (.9m) of thread in the beadwork, and attach the coordinating halves of three snaps at each end of the bracelet (**photo d**).

MATERIALS

bracelet 7½–8½ in. (19.1–21.6cm)

- 49–55 4mm bicone crystals or pearls
- size 11º seed beads
  25–35g color A
  10g color B
- 5g size 15º seed beads
- 3 sew-on snaps, or alternate clasp
- nylon beading thread, size D, conditioned with beeswax or Thread Heaven
- beading needles, #12

Ethnic
echoes

Contrasting colors
and textures define
the feel of this
comfortable peyote
stitch collar

designed by **Virginia Jensen**

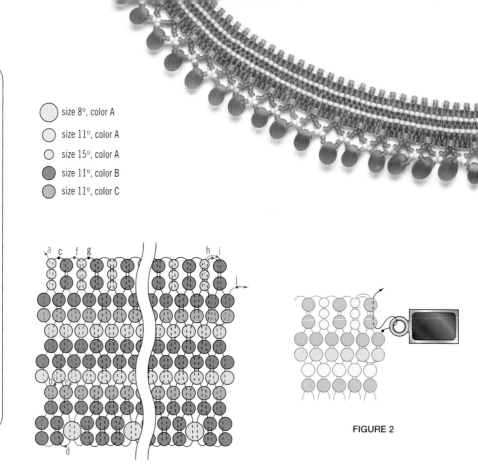

MATERIALS

both collars
- Fireline or Power Pro, 8 lb. test
- beading needles, #10

black-and-white collar
15½ in. (39.4cm)
- **42** 5 x 8mm glass or pearl drop beads
- Japanese seed beads
  2g 8º, color A
  30g 11º, in each of **3** colors: A, B, C
  3g 15º, color A
- clasp

topaz collar 15½ in. (39.4cm)
- **42** 5 x 8mm glass or pearl drop beads
- Japanese seed beads
  1g 8º, color D
  25g 11º, in each of **3** colors: A, B, C
  4g 15º, color B
- clasp

- ◯ size 8º, color A
- ◯ size 11º, color A
- ◯ size 15º, color A
- ◯ size 11º, color B
- ◯ size 11º, color C

FIGURE 1

FIGURE 2

A longtime Egyptophile, Virginia loved the idea of collars. She tried netted collars, but they didn't give her the look she wanted. Eventually she realized that two-drop peyote would give her the design she had envisioned.

stepbystep

Both of these collars begin with a base stitched in modified two-drop peyote. They curve naturally because you stitch 15º seed beads in the inner edge and 8ºs in the outer edge. The curve of the topaz necklace is greater than the black-and-white one because you use 15ºs in every other row along the inner edge, as opposed to every fourth row along the inner edge, as in the black-and-white collar. The pattern shown in figure 1 is for the topaz necklace. For a more gentle curve, substitute two 11ºs for every other group of three 15ºs. Both collars have netting along the outer edge, but the black-and-white collar also has edging along the top and loops across the front. Embellish your collar as desired.

Collar base

[1] On 3 yd. (2.7m) of thread, pick up a stop bead (Basics, p. 10), leaving a 10-in. (25cm) tail. Referring to **figure 1** for the bead pattern, pick up three 15ºs and 12 11ºs. Skip the last four 11ºs, and sew back through the next two (**a–b**). Work two more two-drop peyote stitches using two 11ºs per stitch, and exit the first three 15ºs added (**b–c**).
[2] Work three two-drop peyote stitches, using two 11ºs per stitch (**c–d**).
[3] Work one stitch with an 8º instead of two 11ºs (**d–e**).
[4] Work two two-drop peyote stitches using two 11ºs per stitch (**e–f**).

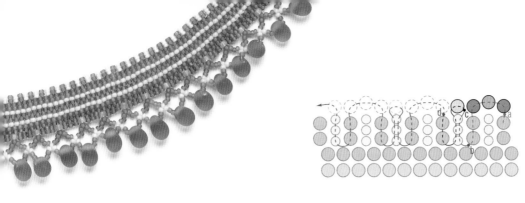

FIGURE 4

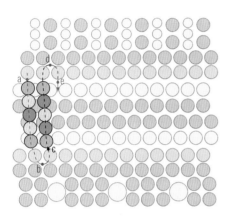

FIGURE 3

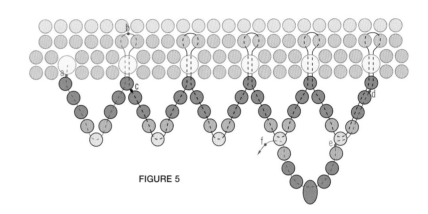

FIGURE 5

[5] Work one stitch using either three 15ºs or two 11ºs, as explained above, and then work five two-drop peyote stitches using 11ºs **(f–g)**.

[6] Continue working in modified two-drop peyote **(g–h)**, adding and ending thread (Basics) as needed until your collar is 14½ in. (36.8cm) or the desired length, keeping the length of the clasp in mind.

[7] Work two more rows of two-drop peyote using 11ºs **(h–i)**. Sew through the beadwork to exit at **point j**.

[8] Pick up half of the clasp, and sew through the next two 11ºs (figure 2). Retrace the thread path several times to reinforce the clasp. End the working thread.

[9] Remove the stop bead from the tail on the other end of the collar, and repeat steps 7–9 to attach the other half of the clasp.

Embellishments
Front loops
[1] Add 2 yd. (1.8m) of thread in the beadwork, and exit at **figure 3, point a**.

[2] Pick up a color C 11º, a color A 11º, a color B 11º, an A 11º, and a C. Skip over four 11ºs on the collar base, and sew through the next C **(a–b)**. Sew through the adjacent C in the horizontal row **(b–c)**.

[3] Pick up a C, a B 11º, an A 11º, a B 11º, and a C. Skip over four 11ºs on the collar base, and sew through the next C **(c–d)**. Sew through the next C **(d–e)**.

[4] Repeat steps 2 and 3 along the center rows of stitches until you reach the other end. End the threads.

Top edge
[1] Add 1 yd. (.9m) of thread in the beadwork, and exit one end of the collar at **figure 4, point a**.

[2] Pick up a B 11º, a C, and a B 11º. Skip the next stack of beads, and sew through the following stack **(a–b)**. Sew through the next stack **(b–c)**.

[3] Pick up an A 11º, and sew back through the stack your thread just exited and through the next stack **(c–d)**.

[4] Repeat steps 2 and 3 along the inner edge until you reach the other end. End the threads.

Netting
[1] Add 2 yd. (1.8m) of thread in the beadwork, and exit the first 8º from one end along the outer edge of stitches **(figure 5, point a)**.

[2] Pick up three B 11ºs, a C, an A 11º, a C, and three B 11ºs. Sew through the next 8º and 11º **(a–b)**. Sew through the adjacent 11º and back through the 8º and the 11º below it **(b–c)**.

[3] Repeat step 2, but pick up only two B 11ºs at first, then pick up the remaining sequence. Repeat along the outer edge until you reach the other end **(c–d)**. When you reach the last stitch, sew back through the previous four 11ºs **(d–e)**.

[4] Pick up a C, two B 11ºs, a drop bead, two B 11ºs, and a C. Sew through the A 11º in the next loop of the previous row of netting **(e–f)**.

[5] Repeat step 4 until you reach the other end. End the threads.

49

Even the odds

Odd-count peyote creates symmetry, while square stitch brings this bracelet to a creative close

designed by **Pamm Horbit**

MATERIALS
bracelet 7¼ in. (18.4cm)
- 12mm accent bead for clasp
- Japanese seed beads
  22g 4mm cubes
  30g size 11º
- nylon beading thread, size D
- beading needles, #12

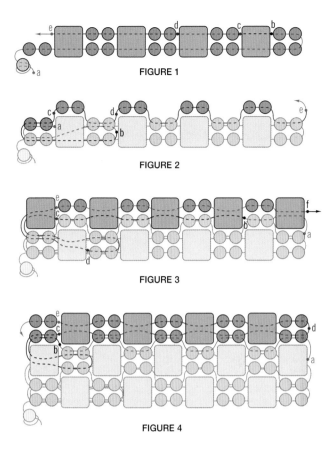

FIGURE 1

FIGURE 2

FIGURE 3

FIGURE 4

Odd-count peyote stitch can be tricky, yet it's essential if you want to incorporate a centered design in your beadwork without changing stitches. The transition from one row to the next can be confusing, and this cuff alternates between regular and two-drop peyote, so it takes a while to master the technique. Once you finish this clever cuff, you'll have another great variation of peyote stitch to add to your repertoire.

stepbystep

Peyote band

[1] Determine the desired length of your bracelet, and subtract 1¾ in. (4.4cm) from it. This will be the length of the peyote band.

[2] On a comfortable length of thread, attach a stop bead (Basics, p. 10), leaving an 18-in. (46cm) tail. Pick up an alternating pattern of two 11º seed beads and a 4mm cube four times, then pick up four 11ºs (figure 1, a–b). Sew back through the last 4mm (b–c). Working in modified flat two-drop peyote stitch (Peyote Basics, p. 5), pick up two 11ºs, and sew through the next 4mm (c–d). Repeat twice (d–e).

[3] Pick up two 11ºs, and sew through the first two 11ºs added in step 1, the next 4mm, and the next two 11ºs (figure 2, a–b). Turn, and sew back through the two 11ºs above the two 11ºs your thread is exiting, the 4mm, and the next four 11ºs (b–c).

[4] Working in two-drop peyote, pick up two 11ºs, skip the 4mm, and sew through the next two 11ºs in the previous row (c–d). Repeat across the row (d–e).

[5] Work the next row in regular peyote (Basics): Pick up a 4mm, and sew through the next two 11ºs in the previous row (figure 3, a–b). Repeat three times (b–c). Pick up a 4mm, and work the odd-count turn by sewing

through the two end 11ºs in the previous row, the 4mm, and the next four 11ºs (c–d). Sew back through the 4mm, two 11ºs, and the 4mm just picked up (d–e).

[6] Work a row of two-drop peyote using 11ºs, sewing through the 4mms in the previous row (e–f).

[7] Work a row of two-drop peyote using 11ºs and sewing through the 11ºs in the previous row (figure 4, a–b). At the end of the row, work the odd-count turn as shown (b–c).

[8] Work a row of regular peyote using 4mms (c–d).

[9] Work a row of two-drop peyote using 11ºs (d–e). When you reach the last stitch, repeat step 3.

[10] Continue alternating rows of two-drop and regular peyote by repeating steps 3–8 until you reach the length determined in step 1. End and add thread (Basics) as needed. Make sure your peyote band has a row with five 4mms at each end, and end the working thread. Leave the tail to sew the accent bead to the end row.

a

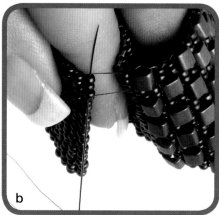

b

c

Square stitch closure

[1] Add a comfortable length of thread at the end of the peyote band without the tail, and exit an edge 4mm in the last row **(figure 5, point a)**.

[2] Work four rows of square stitch (Basics), using three 11ºs for the first and last stitch, and two 11ºs for the stitches in between **(a–b)**.

[3] Continuing in square stitch, refer to **figure 5** to incorporate four 4mms into the pattern.

[4] Continue stitching with 11ºs only until the strip is long enough to fit around the 12mm accent bead **(photo a)**.

[5] Work a square stitch thread path to connect the last row to the first row **(photo b)**, forming a tube.

[6] On the other end of the peyote band, exit an end 4mm. Pick up 37 11ºs, the 12mm, and an 11º. Sew back through the 12mm and the 37 11ºs. Sew back through the last row of the peyote band, exiting the other end 4mm. Pick up enough 11ºs to fit around the 12mm, and sew back through the 4mm **(photo c)**. Retrace the thread path, and end the thread.

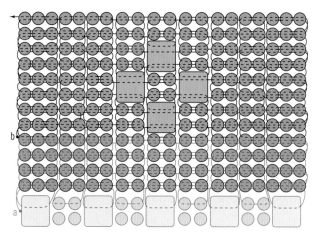

FIGURE 5

EDITOR'S NOTE:
After establishing the first few rows, you can start to work the more simplified odd-count peyote turn (Peyote Basics) by sewing under the previous edge thread bridge and back through the last bead or beads added.

Whirling
peyote

Waves of color wash over glistening crystals

designed by **Kathryn Bowman**

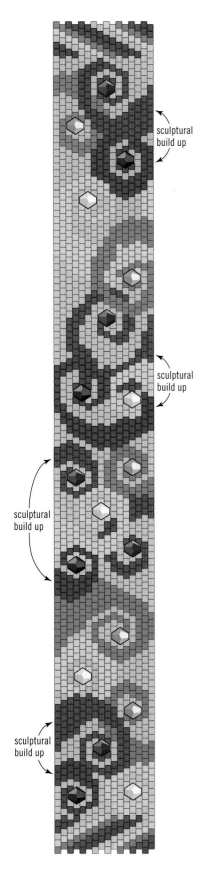

sculptural
build up

sculptural
build up

sculptural
build up

sculptural
build up

FIGURE 1

FIGURE 2

FIGURE 3

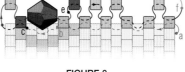

FIGURE 4

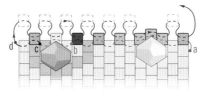

FIGURE 5

Lacy edging, peyote stitch, and a touch of sparkle make a winning combination. Sculptural elements emphasize the fluidity of this easy-to-make bracelet.

step*by*step

Bracelet

[1] On a comfortable length of thread, attach a stop bead (Basics, p. 10), leaving an 8-in. (20cm) tail. Following the pattern from the bottom up (**figure 1**), pick up 16 11º cylinder beads to make up the first two rows, and work even-count peyote stitch (Peyote Basics, p. 5) until you complete 15 rows.

[2] Work the first six stitches of row 16, up to the inclusion (**figure 2, a–b**). To form a window for the 4mm bicone crystal, sew through the next three cylinders in the previous two rows (**b–c**). Follow the pattern to complete the row (**c–d**).

[3] Begin the next row, and, in the space created by the missing cylinder, pick up a bicone and sew through the next cylinder (**d–e**). Complete the row following the pattern. Note: There are several places in this pattern where two bicones are spaced one row apart. In such cases, remember to leave an opening for a bicone, as in **e–f**.

[4] In the next row, continue following the pattern, placing a bicone in the space created in the previous row, stitching up to the first bicone added (**figure 3, a–b**). Sew through the bicone, and continue following the pattern to the end of the row (**b–c**).

[5] In the next row, stitch to the first bicone. Pick up three cylinders, skip over the bicone, sew through the next cylinder on the row, (**c–d**), and continue following the pattern (**d–e**).

[6] In the next row, work up to the three cylinders that are on top of the first bicone (**figure 4, a–b**). Sew through these three cylinders (**b–c**), and continue to the end of the row (**c–d**). Work the next row in normal peyote stitch, following the pattern.

[7] Complete the bracelet following the pattern, working the remaining crystal inclusions as in steps 2–6. Add and end thread (Basics) as necessary. Do not trim the starting tail or working thread, as these will be used to create the pockets.

Sculptural embellishment

Each sculptural embellishment is placed only on those swirls that do not have any swirls overlapping them. Embellishment is at your discretion.

[1] Secure a comfortable length of thread in the beadwork (Basics), and exit at the point where the embellishment will begin.

[2] Begin the layer one cylinder in from the edge of the swirl. Pick up a cylinder, sew through the cylinder directly below where the new cylinder will be placed, and sew through the new cylinder again.

[3] Continue stitching cylinders to the base, following the pattern.

[4] To include a second layer, repeat steps 2 and 3.

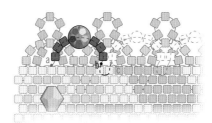

FIGURE 6

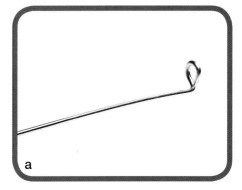

a

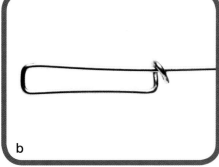

b

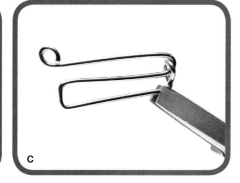

c

Three-layer edging

This edging is worked with three colors of cylinders from the bracelet.

[1] **Layer 1:** Secure a new thread in the beadwork so that it exits 11 rows from the edge. Pick up seven cylinders, skip four edge cylinders, sew into the fifth edge cylinder, and sew up through the next cylinder (**figure 5, a–b**). Repeat for the length of the bracelet.

[2] **Layer 2:** Position the thread so it exits the first open edge cylinder inside the previous loop in layer 1 (**point c**). Pick up two cylinders, sew through the center cylinder of the loop from layer 1 (**c–d**), pick up five cylinders, and sew through the center cylinder again (**d–e**). Pick up two more cylinders, skip two edge cylinders, and sew through the next cylinder (**e–f**). Sew through the beadwork as shown, exiting inside the second loop (**f–g**). Repeat for the length of the bracelet.

[3] **Layer 3:** With the front of the bracelet facing you, position the thread so it exits the second open edge cylinder inside the first loop (**figure 6, point a**). Pick up three cylinders, a 4mm round crystal, and three cylinders. Sew into the first empty edge bead inside the second loop (**a–b**). Sew up through the next cylinder (**b–c**). Repeat for the length of the bracelet. Secure the thread, and trim.

[4] Repeat steps 1–3 on the other edge of the bracelet. Secure the thread, and trim.

Concealed hook and pockets

[1] Cut a 4-in. (10cm) piece of 16-gauge wire.

[2] Make a plain loop (Basics) at one end. Using chainnose pliers, bend the loop up at a right angle to the wire (**photo a**).

[3] Measure the width of the bracelet, and make another right-angle bend this distance from the loop. Make a third bend ⅛ in. (3mm) farther down the wire. Open the loop (Basics), and slip the wire tail into the loop (**photo b**). Close the loop.

[4] Bend the wire tail over the top of the loop so that it is going in the opposite direction. Make a loop at the end of the wire. Using chainnose pliers, bend the loop at a slight angle (**photo c**). This angle will help prevent the hook from sliding out while you are wearing the bracelet.

[5] Fold the striped section at the end of the band to the back of the bracelet, and check that the resulting pocket is large enough for the finished hook to slide through.

[6] Zip (Peyote Basics) the end row to the back side of the bracelet. Secure the thread, and trim.

[7] Remove the stop bead, and slide the other end of the bracelet through the rectangular opening of the hook. Fold the striped section over the clasp, away from the hook. Repeat step 6 using the tail.

MATERIALS
7¾ in. (19.7cm) bracelet
- **20** 4mm bicone crystals in each of **5** colors to match cylinder beads: A, B, C, D, E
- **40** 4mm round crystals or fire-polished beads in one of the above colors
- **7g** 11º Japanese cylinder beads in each of **5** colors: A, B, C, D, E
- **4 in.** (10cm) 16-gauge wire, dead-soft
- nylon beading thread, size D
- beading needles, #12
- chainnose pliers
- roundnose pliers
- wire cutters

One good turn

Stitch a Dutch spiral necklace using seed beads in a variety of sizes and shapes

designed by **Elaine Pinckney**

Here the serpentine look and feel of tubular peyote is enhanced with the simple increases and decreases of the Dutch spiral stitch, creating an undulating wave of color that transforms a sleek peyote tube into an entirely different animal. The hidden snap closure gives the impression that you're wearing one artfully infinite curl.

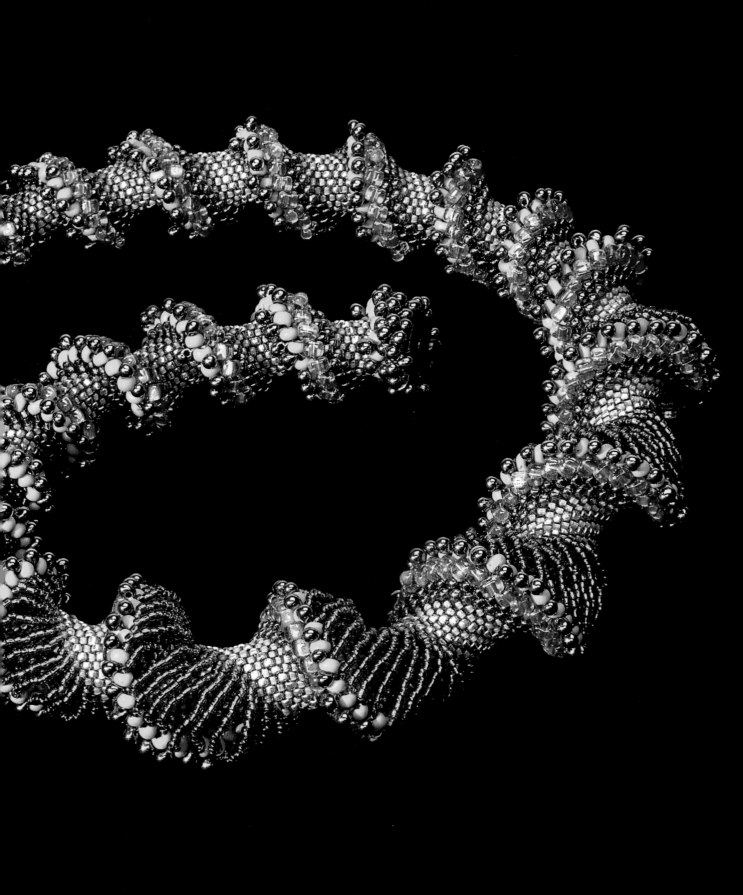

MATERIALS

necklace 19 in. (48cm)

- seed beads
  - 40g 5º triangles, color B
  - 24g 6ºs or 16g 8º hex-cuts or triangles, in **2** colors: C, D
  - 16g 8ºs, color E
  - 15–20g 11ºs, color F
  - 36g 11º, color A
  - 8g 11º rounds, hex-cuts, or triangles in each of **4** colors: G, H, I, J
- 40g 3mm drop beads (optional)
- 15mm metal snap
- Fireline, 8 or 10 lb. test, or nylon beading thread, size B, conditioned with beeswax
- beading needles, #12

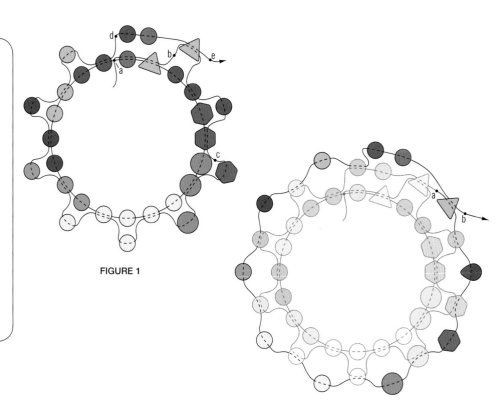

FIGURE 1

FIGURE 2

stepbystep

[1] On a comfortable length of doubled conditioned thread or Fireline, pick up 20 seed beads in the following color sequence: an A, a B, two Cs, two Ds, two Es, four Fs, two Gs, two Hs, two Is, and two Js. Leaving a 6-in. (15cm) tail, tie the beads into a ring with a square knot (Basics, p. 10), and sew through the first two beads again **(figure 1, a–b)**.

[2] Work round 3 in tubular peyote (Peyote Basics, p. 5) as follows: Pick up a B, skip the first C, and sew through the second C. Pick up a C, skip the first D, and sew through the second D **(b–c)**. Continue the pattern around the ring, adding a D, an E, two Fs, a G, an H, and an I **(c–d)**. To step up, pick up a J and an A, and sew through the B added in this round **(d–e)**.

[3] Rounds 4–40: Repeat step 2 **(figure 2, a–b)**.

[4] Continue working the pattern in tubular peyote as in rounds 1–40, adding and ending thread (Basics) as needed, but increase the number of As you pick up at the step-up of each round as follows:

Rounds 41–80: Two As.
Rounds 81–100: Three As.
Rounds 101–105: Four As.
Rounds 106–110: Five As.
Rounds 111–112: Six As.
Rounds 113–114: Seven As.
Rounds 115–116: Eight As.
Rounds 117–118: Nine As.
Rounds 119–120: Ten As.
Rounds 121–122: Eleven As.
Rounds 123–124: Twelve As.
Rounds 125–126: Thirteen As.
Rounds 127–128: Fourteen As.
Rounds 129–247: Fifteen As.

[5] Rounds 129–247 form the center of the necklace. The finished necklace length is 19–19½ in. (48–49.5cm). To increase the length of your necklace, continue adding rounds with 15 As until you have added the desired length.

[6] Decrease the number of As picked up for the following rounds so the second half of the necklace is the mirror image of the first.

Rounds 248–249: Fourteen As.
Rounds 250–251: Thirteen As.
Rounds 252–253: Twelve As.
Rounds 254–255: Eleven As.
Rounds 256–257: Ten As.
Rounds 258–259: Nine As.
Rounds 260–261: Eight As.
Rounds 262–263: Seven As.
Rounds 264–265: Six As.
Rounds 266–270: Five As.
Rounds 271–275: Four As.
Rounds 276–295: Three As.
Rounds 296–335: Two As.
Rounds 336–375: One A.

[7] Sew a snap half to the first and last rounds of the spiral **(photo a)**. Make sure the snap halves are securely attached, and then hide the edges of the snap with a round of peyote, using one of the larger beads from the pattern **(photos b and c)**. End the threads.

If desired, sew into the ridge of Bs, and add a 3mm drop bead between each pair of Bs. This adds detail and accentuates the spiral.

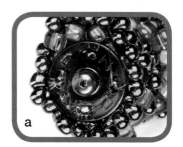

a

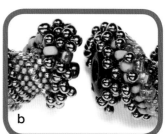

b

c

Jewel-box bracelet

Inspired by the bold jeweled cuffs of the 1940s, this colorful band looks at home on the runway or around your wrist

designed by **Cathy Lampole**

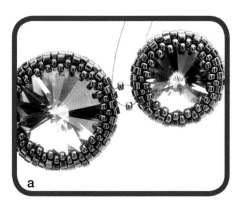

a

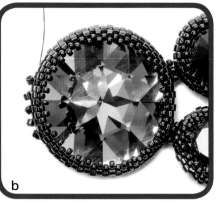

b

Search your collection of "jewels" to find the perfect pieces for this bracelet. Whether you go colorful or monochromatic, it's easy to find the perfect crystals to make your bracelet a standout.

stepbystep

Before you start assembling the bracelet, you may want to gather your rivolis and stones and lay them on a sheet of paper. Arrange them into a pattern you like, placing a large stone at each end to connect to the closure, and trace around them to make a template. Keep in mind that once you bezel the rivolis and stones and start to connect them, you may have to adjust your plans.

Bezels
On 24 in. (61cm) of Fireline, attach a stop bead (Basics, p. 10), leaving a 12-in. (30cm) tail. Using the "Bezeling rivolis" chart (left) as a guide, pick up enough cylinder beads to fit around the rivoli or stone. Work in tubular peyote to bezel the rivoli (Peyote Basics, p. 5), stitching a total of four rows with 11º cylinder beads with two rows of 15º seed beads on each surface of the stone. Do not end the working thread or tail. Repeat to bezel the remaining stones and rivolis.

Connections
Lay out the rivolis and stones as you would like them to sit in the bracelet, using your template as a guide, if you made one. Start at one end of the bracelet and work to the other, using the tails from the bezels to make the connections.
[1] Sew through the bezel of an end rivoli or stone to exit the cylinder in the initial round where you would like to connect the next rivoli or stone. Pick up a 15º, sew through a cylinder in the initial round of the next rivoli or stone, pick up a 15º, and sew through the first cylinder again (photo a). Retrace the thread path several times to reinforce the connection. Sew through an adjacent cylinder on the first bezel and repeat to make a second connection.

[2] Continue connecting the remaining rivolis and stones as in step 1, working from one end of the bracelet to the other. As you make the connections, try to keep the bracelet in a rectangular shape. Each rivoli or stone should connect to at least two others. When all the rivolis and stones are connected, end all the threads (Basics).

Clasp
[1] Add a new thread (Basics) to the outer edge of a large stone bezel at one end of the bracelet, exiting a cylinder in the initial round about five cylinders from the center of the edge. Working in peyote stitch, work five stitches across the edge of the bezel (photo b).
[2] Turn, and work in flat even-count peyote stitch (Peyote Basics) for 26 rows. To decrease the tab to a point, turn, and sew through the adjacent edge cylinder and the next cylinder (figure 1, a–b). Turn, and sew through the adjacent cylinder, the next two edge cylinders, and the last cylinder added (b–c). Work back across the row in peyote stitch, and repeat the turn at the opposite end (c–d). Continue decreasing each row until the tab comes to a point (d–e).
[3] Sew through the beadwork to exit an edge cylinder where the tab meets the bezel. Pick up two 15ºs, and sew through both 15ºs again (figure 2, a–b). Sew under the thread bridge between the next edge cylinder and the cylinder after, and sew back through the second 15º (b–c). Continue working in brick stitch (Basics) along the length of the edge.
[4] To add 15ºs to the tapered point, pick up a 15º, and sew through the previous 15º and the new 15º again (figure 3, a–b). Pick up a 15º, and sew through the next cylinder and the new 15º again (b–c). Continue working in modified square stitch (Basics) around the point of the tab, then use brick stitch to add 15ºs to the other edge.

BEZELING RIVOLIS: HOW MANY CYLINDERS DO I PICK UP?
It can be challenging to guess how many cylinders fit in the initial bezel ring, which makes up the first two rounds of peyote. The initial ring should always have an even number of beads and fit around the widest part of your rivoli or stone. Here are some estimates for the number of cylinders needed to make these initial rings.

Size of rivoli/ stone	Number of 11º cylinders
12mm	30
12 x 18mm	40
14mm	36
16mm	40
18mm	46
22 x 30mm	64
27mm	68

MATERIALS
bracelet 7½–9 in. (19.1–23cm)
- 10–12 12–32mm crystal rivolis or stones in a variety of shapes and sizes
- 16mm rivoli button
- 25 4mm bicone crystals
- 8g 11º Japanese cylinder beads
- 5g 15º Japanese seed beads
- Fireline, 6 lb. test
- beading needles, #12 or #13

[5] Sew through the beadwork to exit the center of the tab, 10 rows from the tip. Pick up two 15°s, a rivoli button, and two 15°s, and sew back into the beadwork where the thread exited. Sew through the beadwork, and retrace the thread path several times to secure the button. End the thread.

[6] Repeat step 1 at the opposite end of the bracelet to start the other half of the clasp. Turn, and work seven rows of peyote stitch with cylinders (figure 4, a–b). Turn, work two stitches (b–c), turn, and work back across the row (c–d). Continue working two stitches per row for 22 more rows (d–e).

[7] Add a second thread to the beadwork, and exit the tab at **point y**. Work two peyote stitches per row for 24 rows (y–z).

[8] Using the thread from step 6, work two stitches, pick up three cylinders, and sew through the next up-bead in the strip from step 7 (e–f). Work the final stitch of the row, turn, and work a row of regular peyote (f–g). Taper the point as in step 2 (g–h).

[9] Use the tail from step 7 to secure the join between the two strips, and end the thread.

[10] Repeat steps 3 and 4 to edge the second half of the clasp with 15°s. Exit the last 15° of the edging.

[11] Pick up a 15°, a 4mm bicone crystal, and a 15°. Skip the last 15°, and sew back through the 4mm (figure 5, a–b). Pick up a 15°, and sew through the next two 15°s (b–c). Repeat along the straight edges, and along the tapered point, as shown in **figure 6**. End the threads.

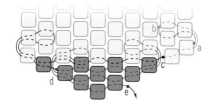

FIGURE 1

FIGURE 2

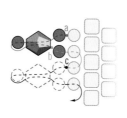

FIGURE 3

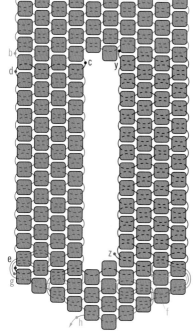

FIGURE 4

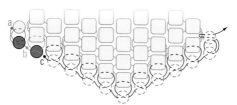

FIGURE 5

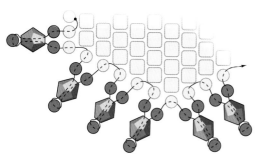

FIGURE 6

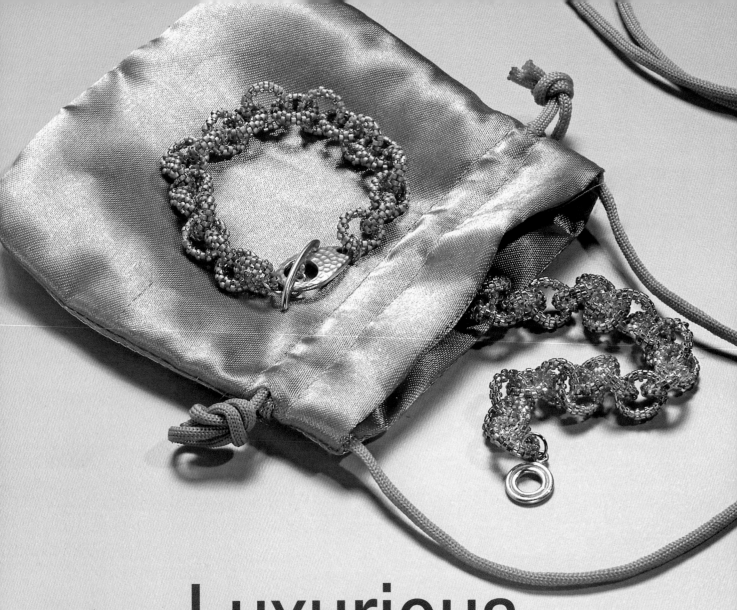

Luxurious links

designed by **Anna Elizabeth Draeger**

Tubular peyote loops link up for a classy bracelet

MATERIALS
bracelet 7 in. (18cm)
- 10g 11º Japanese cylinder beads
- 8g 15º Japanese seed beads
- clasp
- 2 5mm inside diameter (ID) jump rings
- 4mm ID jump ring (optional)
- Fireline, 6 lb. test
- beading needles, #12
- chainnose pliers
- roundnose pliers

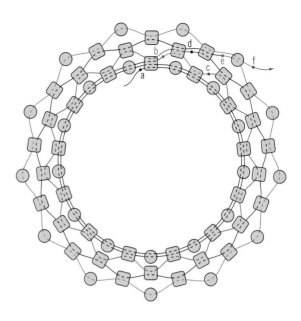

FIGURE

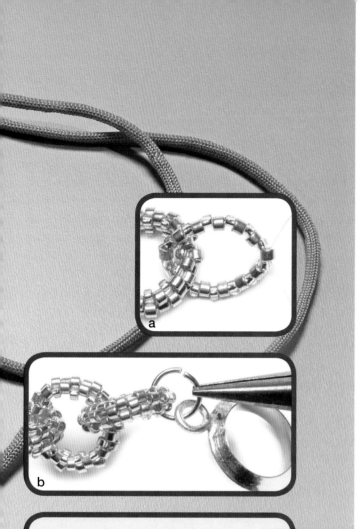

DESIGNER'S NOTES:

• If you are using a toggle and loop clasp, you may have to use an extra 4mm jump ring to attach the toggle bar. This extra length will allow the toggle bar to pivot enough to get through the loop.

• Use different colors to change the look of the links from dressy to casual.

To mimic expensive, chunky metal chain, Anna worked tubular peyote stitch with cylinders and seed beads. This textured reproduction is lightweight and easy to wear.

step by step

[1] On 1 yd. (.9m) of Fireline, pick up an alternating pattern of an 11º cylinder bead and a 15º seed bead until you have 26 beads, leaving a 6-in. (15cm) tail. Sew through all the beads again to form a ring, and exit the first cylinder (figure 1, a–b).

[2] Work a round of tubular peyote (Peyote Basics, p. 5) using cylinders: Pick up a cylinder, skip a 15º in the ring, and sew through the next cylinder (b–c). Repeat to complete the round, and step up through the first cylinder in the new round (c–d).

[3] Work a round of tubular peyote using cylinders (d–e).

[4] Work a round of tubular peyote using 15º s (e–f), pulling the round snug.

[5] Sew back through each round to reinforce the link, working back to the tail.

[6] Tie the working thread and the tail together with a surgeon's knot (Basics, p. 10). Sew through several beads with each tail, and trim.

[7] To make subsequent links, repeat steps 1–6, but before forming the ring in step 1, pass the row of cylinders through the previous ring (photo a).

[8] Continue to make links until your chain is the desired length, minus the length of the clasp.

[9] Open a 5mm jump ring (Basics). Slide the last link of the beaded chain and one half of the clasp on the jump ring (photo b), and close the jump ring. Repeat with the other half of the clasp.

Ropes and rings

A network of connected rings showcases the sparkle of crystal and the luster of pearls

designed by **Laura McCabe**

a

b

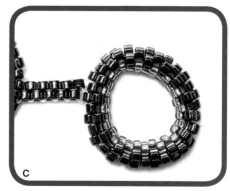

c

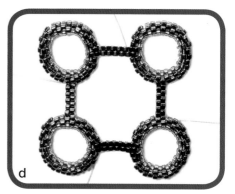

d

Inspired by the opulence of late 18th century French jewelry and apparel, this bracelet pairs richly colored crystal stones and metallic Charlottes with two strands of freshwater pearls that wind through the outer rings to frame bezel-set rivolis.

stepbystep

End and add Fireline (Basics, p. 10) as needed.

Rings

[1] On 1 yd. (.9m) of Fireline, pick up 32 15º seed beads, and, leaving a 12-in. (30cm) tail, sew through the first few 15ºs again to form a ring. Using 15ºs, work a round in tubular peyote stitch (Peyote Basics, p. 5), and step up.
[2] Work three rounds in tubular peyote using 11º cylinder beads.
[3] Thread a needle on the tail, and work two rounds using cylinders.
[4] Zip up (Peyote Basics) the last round of cylinders added in step 3 and the last round of cylinders added in step 2. Tie a few half-hitch knots (Basics) to secure the thread, but do not trim.
[5] Repeat steps 1–4 to make a total of 18 rings.

Stone bezels

[1] Sew through the beadwork of a ring to exit a cylinder in the first round of cylinders. Work two rounds of tubular peyote using cylinders **(photo a)**, and step up.
[2] Place a 12mm rivoli or cubic zirconia stone in the bezel face up, and work a round of tubular peyote with 15º seed beads. Work another round using 15º Czech Charlottes. Tie half-hitch knots to secure the thread, but do not trim.
[3] Sew through the beadwork to exit a cylinder in the first round on the back side

of the bezel. Work two rounds with 15º seed beads. Work a round with 15º Czech Charlottes. Tie a few half-hitch knots to secure the thread, but do not trim.
[4] Repeat steps 1–3 to make a total of five stone bezels.

Linking components

[1] Sew through the beadwork of a ring to exit a cylinder in the outer center round. Work a peyote stitch using a cylinder. Pick up a cylinder, turn, and sew through the cylinder just added **(photo b)**. Working in flat even-count peyote (Peyote Basics), make a strip that is two cylinders wide by 10 rows long with five cylinders on each edge. Zip up the last two rows of the strip to the outer center round of cylinders in a new ring **(photo c)**.
[2] Connect two more rings to the first two rings in the same manner, stitching the strips at right angles to form the four rings into a square. There should be six cylinders between each pair of strips on a ring to form the right angle **(photo d)**.
[3] Continuing in the pattern of groups of four, connect 12 rings in this manner for the length of the bracelet.
[4] To add picots along the edges of the strips, sew through the beadwork to exit the first cylinder on a strip. Pick up three 15º Czech Charlottes, and sew through the next two cylinders. Repeat **(photo e)** to add picots along both edges of the strip. Add picot trim to all the strips except the end strips, which is where the clasp will be attached.

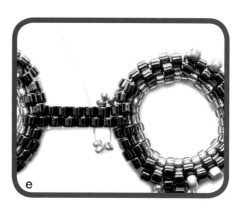

e

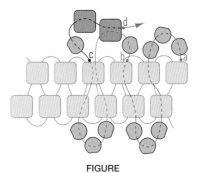

FIGURE

[5] To embellish each ring, work a round of peyote stitch off the second round of cylinders using 15º Japanese Charlottes (**photo f**).

[6] To add a bezel-set stone, use the tail from the bezel to work a strip as in step 1 that is two beads wide by two rows long with one cylinder on each edge. Align the strip with the "corner" of a ring in a square of rings, and zip up the strip to the ring (**photo g**). Add picot trim to the strip as in step 4. Work three more strips around the bezel-set stone at right angles to each other with six cylinders between each pair of strips.

[7] Sew through the beadwork to exit the top round of cylinders in the bezel, and work a round using 15º Japanese Charlottes. Sew through the beadwork to exit the round below the one you worked at the start of this step, and work a round of picots with three 15º Czech Charlottes in each stitch (**photo h**).

[8] Repeat steps 6 and 7 with the remaining bezel-set stones.

Toggle clasp

[1] Sew through the beadwork to exit an end cylinder on an end strip, and work two picots with Czech Charlottes

(**figure, a–b**). Pick up a Czech Charlotte and a cylinder, sew down through the next two cylinders, add a picot, and sew up through the next cylinder and the cylinder you just sewed down through (**b–c**). Pick up a Czech Charlotte and a cylinder, and sew through the first cylinder added (**c–d** and **photo i**). Working in flat even-count peyote stitch and using the two cylinders just added, make a strip that is two cylinders wide by 10 rows long with five cylinders on each edge.

[2] Repeat step 1 on the other end of the bracelet, making a strip that is two

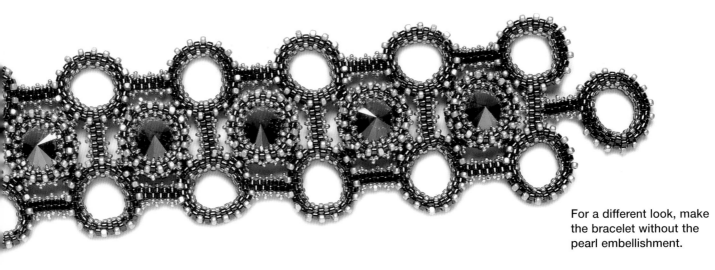

For a different look, make the bracelet without the pearl embellishment.

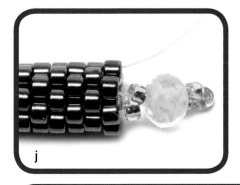

j

k

MATERIALS
bracelet 6¼ in. (15.9cm)
- **5** 12mm rivolis or cubic zirconia stones with pointed backs
- **2** 4mm rondelles
- **2** 16-in. (41cm) strands 3mm freshwater pearls
- 15g 11º cylinder beads
- 6g 15º seed beads
- 6g 15º Japanese Charlottes
- 5g 15º Czech Charlottes
- Fireline, 6 lb. test
- beading needles, #12 and #13
- beading wax (optional)

DESIGNER'S NOTES:
- **Adjust the size of your bracelet by using more rings and 12mm rivolis or stones. A bracelet made with 21 rings and six stones measures about 7 in. (18cm). For a 7¾-in. (19.7cm) bracelet, use 24 rings and seven stones. You may need an extra strand of pearls.**
- **Use 2 yd. (1.8m) of Fireline to make the rings that you will use as bezels for the stones.**
- **Depending on your tension and the manufacturer of your rivolis or stones, when stitching the bezel, you may need to work an extra round with 15º seed beads before switching to 15º Czech Charlottes.**

cylinders wide by 18 rows long with nine cylinders on each edge.

[3] Using the thread of the remaining unattached ring, sew through the beadwork to exit a cylinder in the outer round. Work a round with Japanese Charlottes, leaving one cylinder unembellished. Using the unembellished bead, zip up the ring to the 10-row strip made in step 1. Sew through the beadwork to exit an end cylinder on the strip, and work picots along the edges with Czech Charlottes. Add picots to the remaining edge of the remaining section of the end strip on the bracelet.

[4] On 1 yd. (.9m) of Fireline, use cylinders to work a strip of peyote that is 12 rows wide by 12 rows long with six cylinders on each edge. Zip up the ends to form a tube.

[5] Sew through the beadwork to exit a cylinder at the end of the tube. Pick up a 15º, a 4mm rondelle, and three 15ºs. Skip the three 15ºs, and sew back through the 4mm. Pick up a 15º, and sew down through the next cylinder and up through the following cylinder (**photo j**). Pick up a 15º, and sew through the 4mm, three 15ºs, and back through the 4mm. Continue in this manner around the end of the tube, and repeat on the other side. End the thread and tail.

[6] Using the thread on the 18-row strip at the end of the bracelet, zip up the strip to the center of the toggle bar. Add picots to the edges of the strip as in step 3. End all threads.

Pearl embellishment
[1] On 1 yd. (.9m) of Fireline, attach a stop bead (Basics), leaving a 6-in. (15cm) tail. String about 15 in. (38cm) of 3mm freshwater pearls. Using the strand of pearls, sew up through a ring on the edge of the bracelet from back to front. Continue weaving the pearl strand through the rings around the bracelet in the same manner, from back to front (**photo k**).

[2] Remove the stop bead, and add or remove pearls as needed. Sew through the first few pearls added, and tie a half-hitch knot. Sew through a few more pearls, and tie a half-hitch knot. Repeat about six times, and end the thread and tail.

[3] Repeat steps 1 and 2 with a second strand of pearls, making sure to keep the second strand around the outer edge of the first strand.

Mimic fine needlework

Staggered rows of two-drop peyote make a striking necklace

designed by **Rebecca Peapples**

Bargello, also called "flame stitch" because its characteristic zigzag pattern resembles flames, is an Italian upholstery and needlework stitch from the 17th century. In this dramatic neckpiece, Rebecca has gracefully re-created the bargello effect using two-drop peyote.

MATERIALS
necklace 20 in. (51cm)

- **23–30** 4mm round or drop-shaped glass, pearl, or gemstone beads
- 11º Japanese cylinder beads
  10g color A
  7g color B
  7g color C
- 3g 11º Czech seed beads, color A or B
- 3g 15º Japanese seed beads, color C
- 10mm bead for clasp
- nylon beading thread, size B or D, conditioned with beeswax or Thread Heaven
- beading needles, #12

FIGURE 1

FIGURE 2

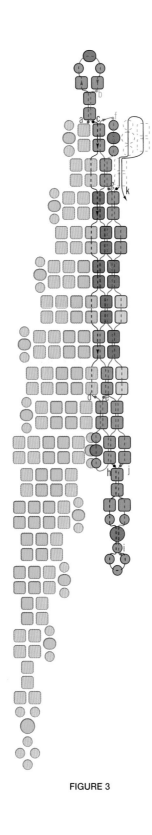

FIGURE 3

FIGURE 4

stepbystep

Getting started

[1] Attach a stop bead (Basics, p. 10) to 2–4 yd. (1.8–3.7m) of conditioned thread, and, leaving a 1–2-yd. (.9–1.8m) tail.

[2] Pick up a 15º seed bead, an 11º seed bead, a 15º, four color A 11º cylinder beads, eight color B 11º cylinders, and four As (figure 1, a–b).

[3] Pick up an A, a 15º, a 4mm round bead, and four 15ºs (b–c). Sew back through the first of the four 15ºs and the 4mm (c–d). Pick up a 15º and an A, and sew through the last two As from the previous step (d–e). (If you're using top-drilled drop beads, simply pick up an A, a 15º, a drop bead, a 15º, and an A, and go back through the last two As from the previous step.)

[4] Work four stitches in two-drop peyote (Peyote Basics, p. 5), using a pair of As, a pair of Bs, a pair of Bs, and a pair of As. On the last stitch, sew through the first three beads picked up in step 2 (e–f).

Necklace

[1] Pick up two As, a 15º, an 11º, a 15º, and two As, and sew back through the first two As just picked up (figure 2, a–b). This sequence will be referred to as a long turn.

[2] Work four stitches in two-drop peyote using the same A, B, B, A sequence used in step 4 of "Getting started" (b–c).

[3] Pick up a 15º, an 11º, and a 15º, and go back through the last two As added in the previous step (c–d). This sequence will be referred to as a short turn.

[4] Work four stitches in two-drop peyote using the A, B, B, A sequence. After

picking up the last two As, sew through the second pair of As from the long turn (d–e).

[5] Repeat steps 1–4 three times.

[6] Pick up three As, a 15º, an 11º, a 15º, and an A (figure 3, a–b), and sew through the first two As just picked up (b–c). This sequence will be referred to as an apex unit.

[7] Work four stitches in two-drop peyote, using the A, B, B, A sequence (c–d). Make a long turn (d–e), and work four two-drop stitches using the A, B, B, A sequence (e–f).

[8] Work a short turn (f–g), then work four two-drop stitches using the A, B, B, A sequence (g–h).

[9] Pick up three As, a 15º, a 4mm, and four 15ºs (h–i). Sew back through the first of the four 15ºs and the 4mm, pick up a 15º and an A, and sew back through the first two As picked up in this step (i–j). This sequence will be referred to as a drop unit.

[10] Work four stitches in two-drop peyote, but substitute color C cylinders for the Bs (j–k). Repeat steps 1–9 using Cs instead of Bs. After making the next drop unit, switch back to using Bs. Continue working in this pattern, alternating Bs and Cs, until the first half of your necklace is the desired length, ending and adding thread (Basics) as needed. End with an apex unit, and embellish the edge with short-turn bead groups, if desired.

[11] To make the other half, flip your work, and remove the stop bead. Thread a needle on the tail, and repeat steps 1–10. After stitching two rows (figure 4, a–b), you may want to reinforce the center point. To do so, weave through the beadwork to exit the top of the 11º used in the first long turn of the first side (b–c). Pick up an 11º, and sew through the 11º and 15º of the first long turn made in this step (c–d). Retrace the thread path a few times, zigzag back to where you left off, and resume stitching the rest of the second side.

Clasp

[1] Exit an A near the top of either end. Pick up two 15ºs, an 11º, the clasp bead, and an 11º. Sew back through the clasp bead and the first 11º picked up. Pick up two 15ºs, and sew through the A adjacent to the one your thread is exiting. Retrace the thread path a few times, and end the thread.

[2] Use the tail on the other end to make a loop. Pick up three 15ºs, an 11º, and enough 15ºs to fit around the clasp bead. Sew back through the 11º (photo a). Pick up three 15ºs, and sew through the A adjacent to the one your thread is exiting (photo b). End the thread.

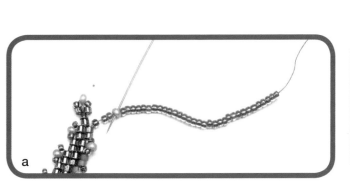

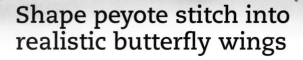

Wing it

Shape peyote stitch into realistic butterfly wings

designed by **Antonio Calles**

Improve your peyote stitch skills by making these beautiful butterfly wings. Master the four different turns — odd-count, even-count, increase, and decrease — and you'll soon be a peyote whiz, able to make any shape you desire.

stepbystep

Large wing

[1] Attach a stop bead (Basics, p. 10) to the center of 1½ yd. (1.4m) of Fireline or thread.

[2] Work the large wing in peyote stitch (Peyote Basics, p. 5), paying close attention to the turn at the end of each row, and referring to **figure 1** to pick up the following 11º seed beads:

Rows 1 and 2: (Outlined in blue in **figure 1**) Two Bs, two As, two Bs, A, three Bs, two Cs, two Bs, two As, two Bs, A, B, three As, B **(a–b)**. Using another needle, pass through every other bead, starting with the last B picked up **(photo a)**. This will help keep your beads in place as you stitch the next row or two.

[3] Work an even-count peyote turn (see turn legend below) to start row 3.

Row 3: B, A, B, two As, four Bs, three As **(b–c)**. Work an even-count turn.

Row 4: B, A, two Bs, A, five Bs, A, B. Work a decrease turn **(c–d and below)**.

Row 5: B, two As, B, five As, B, A. Work an increase turn (see below) by picking up a B and an A, and sewing through them both again, positioning the two beads next to each other **(d–e)**.

Row 6: A, B, A, B, two As, B, two As, two Bs. Pick up another B, and work an odd-count peyote turn **(e–f and below)**.

Row 7: Four Bs, A, two Bs, A, B, two As. Sew through the next A, pick up two Bs, and sew back through the previous A **(f–g)**.

Row 8: A, B, two As, seven Bs. Decrease turn **(g–h)**.

Row 9: Three Cs, B, two Cs, two Bs, two As, B. Work two increase stitches: Pick up two Bs, sew through the first B again, pick up two Bs, and sew through both Bs again so they sit side by side. Sew through the second B in the first stitch **(h–i)**.

Row 10: C, 10 Bs. Pick up a B, and work an odd-count turn **(i–j)**.

Row 11: Three Bs, C, three Bs, C, four Bs **(j–k)**. Even-count turn.

Row 12: Six Bs. Skip the next two stitches by sewing through four Bs **(k–l)**. Two Bs. Work a decrease turn **(l–m)**.

Row 13: B **(m–n)**. Sew through the next six Bs **(n–o)**. B, three Cs, B. Decrease turn **(o–p)**.

Row 14: Four Bs. Decrease turn **(p–q)**.

Row 15: Three Bs **(q–r)**. End the working thread (Basics).

[4] Remove the stop bead, and thread a needle on the tail. Work a decrease turn **(a–s)**, and complete the wing as follows:

Row 16: B, A, five Bs, two As, B, A. Work an increase turn by picking up two Bs **(s–t)**.

Row 17: Three As, two Bs, A, B, C, B, A, B. Decrease turn **(t–u)**.

Row 18: Three Bs, C, two As, three Bs, A. Sew through the next B, and work an odd-count turn **(u–v)**.

Row 19: Three As, B, two As, B, C, two Bs. Decrease turn **(v–w)**.

Row 20: Two Bs, C, three As, two Bs, two As. Work an increase turn by

FOUR TURNS YOU NEED TO KNOW

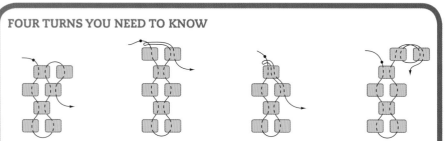

EVEN-COUNT　　ODD-COUNT　　DECREASE　　INCREASE

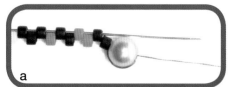

a

MATERIALS

pin 4 x 2 in. (10 x 5cm)

- **2** 8º seed beads (silver-lined)
- 11º seed beads

  3g color A (orange) (Use a slightly darker shade of orange for the large wings and a lighter shade for the smaller wings if desired.)

  5g color B (black)

  2g color C (white)

  1g color D (bronze)
- pin-back finding
- Fireline 4 lb. test or nylon beading thread
- beading needles, #12

picking up two Bs. Sew through the two Bs again, then sew through the last A picked up **(w–x)**.

Row 21: A, B, four As, three Bs. Decrease turn **(x–y)**.

Row 22: Three Bs, two As, B, A, B, A. Work two increase stitches using two Bs for each stitch **(y–z)**. Step up through the second B of the first increase stitch.

Row 23: Three As, B, three As, two Bs. Decrease turn **(z–aa)**.

Row 24: Two Bs, three As, two Bs, two As **(aa–bb)**. Even-count turn.

Row 25: B, two As, B, three As, two Bs. Decrease turn **(bb–cc)**.

Row 26: Two Bs, three As, B, two As **(cc–dd)**. Even-count turn.

Row 27: B, A, B, three As, two Bs. Decrease turn **(dd–ee)**.

Row 28: Two Bs, three As, B, A **(ee–ff)**. Even-count turn.

Row 29: B, four As, two Bs. Decrease turn **(ff–gg)**.

Row 30: Two Bs, two As, B, A **(gg–hh)**. Even-count turn.

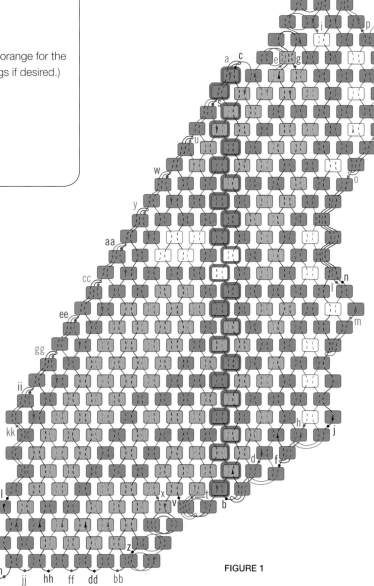

FIGURE 1

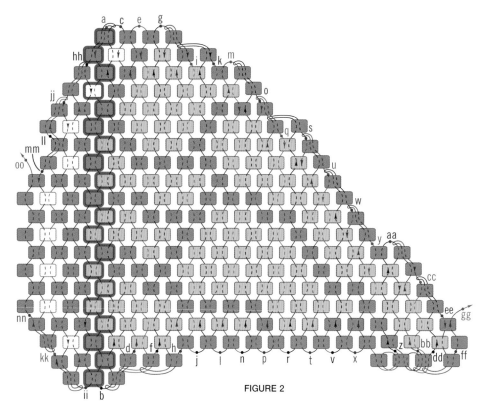

FIGURE 2

Row 31: Two Bs, two As, two Bs. Decrease turn **(hh–ii).**
Row 32: Three Bs, A, B **(ii–jj).** Even-count turn.
Row 33: Five Bs. Decrease turn **(jj–kk).**
Row 34: Skip two stitches by sewing back through the next four Bs **(kk–ll).** Two Bs **(ll–mm).** End the tail.
[5] Make a second large wing.

Small wing

[1] Attach a stop bead to 1½ yd. (1.4m) of Fireline or thread, leaving a 12-in. (30cm) tail.
[2] Work the small wing in peyote stitch as follows, referring to **figure 2:**
Rows 1 and 2: (Outlined in blue in **figure 2**) Three Bs, C, two Bs, A, B, A, B, two As, B, four As, three Bs **(a–b).** Even-count turn.
Row 3: B, two As, B, A, B, A, two Bs, C **(b–c).** Even-count turn.
Row 4: Two Bs, A, B, two As, B, two As, B. Decrease turn **(c–d).**
Row 5: Two As, B, A, two Bs, two As, B **(d–e).** Even-count turn.
Row 6: B, four As, B, A, B, A, B. Odd-count turn **(e–f).**
Row 7: Two As, B, two As, B, three As **(f–g).** Even-count turn.
Row 8: B, four As, three Bs, A, B. Odd-count turn **(g–h).**
Row 9: Two Bs, A, B, A, B, two As, B. Decrease turn **(h–i).**

Row 10: Two As, B, A, B, three As **(i–j).** Even-count turn.
Row 11: Two Bs, two As, three Bs, A, B. Odd-count turn **(j–k).**
Row 12: Two Bs, A, B, four As **(k–l).** Even-count turn.
Row 13: Two Bs, two As, B, three As **(l–m).** Even-count turn.
Row 14: Two Bs, six As **(m–n).** Even-count turn.
Row 15: Two Bs, two As, B, two As, B. Decrease turn **(n–o).**
Row 16: B, two As, B, two As, B **(o–p).** Even-count turn.
Row 17: B, five As, B. Decrease turn **(p–q).**
Row 18: Two As, B, three As **(q–r).** Even-count turn.
Row 19: B, two As, B, two As, B. Odd-count turn **(r–s).**
Row 20: B, two As, B, two As **(s–t).** Even-count turn.
Row 21: B, A, B, two As, B. Decrease turn **(t–u).**
Row 22: B, two As, two Bs **(u–v).** Even-count turn.

Row 23: B, three As, B. Decrease turn **(v–w).**
Row 24: B, A, two Bs **(w–x).** Even-count turn.
Row 25: Two Bs, A, B. Decrease turn **(x–y).**
Row 26: B, A, B. Work an increase stitch using two Bs **(y–z).**
Row 27: B, two As **(z–aa).** Even-count turn.
Row 28: B, two As. Sew through the increase B from the previous turn, pick up a B, and sew through the previous B and the new B **(aa–bb).**
Row 29: Two As, B. Decrease turn **(bb–cc).**
Row 30: B, A. Sew through the next B. Odd-count turn **(cc–dd).**
Row 31: A, B. Decrease turn **(dd–ee).**
Row 32: Two Bs. Odd-count turn **(ee–ff).**
Row 33: B **(ff–gg).**
[3] End the working thread. Remove the stop bead, and thread a needle on the tail. Work a decrease turn **(a–hh),** and complete the wing as follows:
Row 34: Nine Bs **(hh–ii).** Even-count turn.
Row 35: B, C, four Bs, two Cs, B. Decrease turn **(ii–jj).**
Row 36: Eight Bs. Decrease turn **(jj–kk).**
Row 37: B, four Cs, two Bs. Decrease turn **(kk–ll).**
Row 38: Skip a stitch by sewing through the next two beads **(ll–mm).** Five Bs. Decrease turn **(mm–nn).**
Row 39: Four Bs **(nn–oo).** End the tail.
[4] Make a second small wing.

Assembly

[1] On 18 in. (46cm) of thread, work a ladder stitch (Basics) strip three color D 11⁰ seed beads tall, and nine rows long. Repeat to make a second strip, but make it only eight rows long, then work a single D in the center of the ninth row using ladder stitch.
[2] Lay out the ladder stitch strips between the sets of wings **(photo b).** Align the top of the large wings with the top row, and stitch the strip to the wings using a ladder stitch thread path, stitching through the ladder and the edge beads in the wings. Align the second strip between the indentations of the small wings, and stitch them together in the same manner.

> **EDITOR'S NOTE:**
> Using 11⁰ cylinder beads instead of seed beads will result in a slightly smaller butterfly. If you really want to challenge yourself, try using 15⁰s.

[3] Exit the top row of ladder stitch between the two large wings. Pick up an 8º seed bead, an 11º, and an 8º, and sew through the first ladder row again, and continue through the first 8º **(photo c)**.

[4] Pick up 16 Bs, skip the last B, and sew back through the remaining Bs, the 8º, the top three beads in the ladder strip, and the other 8º **(photo d)**. Repeat to make the second antenna.

[5] Stitch the large wings to the small wings by first sewing through the last three beads in the ladder stitch strip between the large wings. Sew through the three beads in the top row of the ladder stitch strip between the small wings **(photo e)**. Retrace the thread path, and tack the two sets of wings together until they're secure.

[6] Position the pin-back finding on the underside of the butterfly **(photo f)**, and tack it down until it is secure by sewing through the holes on the finding and the corresponding beads in the butterfly. End all of the threads.

Galaxy
BEAD

Peyote components
create a beaded bead
that is out of this world

designed by **Gill Slone**

The materials list is for the
necklace with three beaded
beads. To cut down on time and
materials, try making a necklace
with a single focal bead.

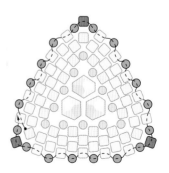

Beaders everywhere will think of the stars and planets when making Gill's galaxy bead. Gill added even more sparkle by using crystals at each connection point.

stepbystep

Components

[1] On 1 yd. (.9m) of Fireline, attach a stop bead (Basics, p. 10), leaving a 12-in. (30cm) tail. Pick up an alternating pattern of a color A 11º cylinder bead and nine color B 11º cylinder beads three times. Sew through the first A to form a ring.

[2] Using Bs, work a round of tubular peyote stitch (Peyote Basics, p. 5), and step up through the first B in the new round **(figure 1)**.

[3] Work four stitches using As, then work a decrease by sewing through the next up-bead. Repeat twice, and step up through the first A **(figure 2)**. This round will pull the beadwork into a rounded triangular shape.

[4] Work a round of peyote using color C 15º seed beads, and step up **(figure 3)**.

[5] Sew through the next two beads to exit the center C on one side of the triangle. Pick up a 4mm bicone crystal, skip three Cs, and sew through the next center C. Repeat twice **(figure 4)**, then retrace the thread path through the beads in the last two rounds, pulling tight to snug up the beads. End the thread (Basics).

[6] Remove the stop bead, and sew through the next outside B. Work four stitches of peyote using color D 15º seed beads. When you reach the corner of the triangle, pick up a D, an A, and a D, and sew through the next B. Repeat twice **(figure 5)**.

[7] Repeat steps 1–6 to make a total of eight components for each beaded bead, but for three of the components, use 2 yd. (1.8m) of Fireline, leaving a 1-yd. (.9m) tail. These tails will be used to assemble the beads.

FIGURE 1

FIGURE 2

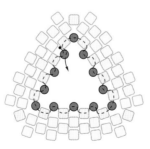

FIGURE 3

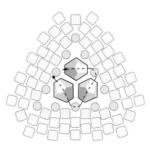

FIGURE 4

FIGURE 5

MATERIALS

necklace with three beaded beads 18 in. (46cm)

- **4** 8mm bicone crystals
- **8** 8mm accent beads
- **138** 4mm bicone crystals
- **4–5g** 11º cylinder beads in each of **2** colors: A, B
- **3–4g** 15º seed beads in each of **2** colors: C, D
- **16** 4mm daisy spacers
- clasp
- **2** 3–4mm jump rings
- **2** crimp beads
- **2** crimp covers
- **2** Wire Guardians
- Fireline, 6 lb. test
- flexible beading wire, .014
- beading needles, #12
- chainnose pliers
- crimping pliers
- wire cutters

Bead assembly

[1] Arrange four components on your work surface with four corner As together. Using a 1-yd. (.9m) tail, sew through to exit the next corner A. Sew through the center corner A in the next three components, then sew through the first A in the first component and the first D. Work five peyote stitches using Ds, and exit the next corner A **(figure 6)**.

[2] Lay the next two components out, and sew through the four corner As. Sew through the next D, and work five peyote stitches using Ds **(figure 7)**. Repeat to connect the last two components.

[3] Sew through the beadwork to exit the last D added, and zip up (Peyote Basics) the two adjacent sides **(figure 8)**. Continue around the bead, either adding a row of Ds and zipping up the sides or just zipping up the sides where the extra row of Ds is already in place, until all the sides are connected. End the threads (Basics).

[4] Repeat steps 1–3 to assemble the remaining beaded beads.

Necklace assembly

[1] On 24 in. (61cm) of beading wire, string a crimp bead, a 4mm bicone crystal, and a Wire Guardian. Go back through the 4mm and the crimp bead, and crimp it (Basics). Use chainnose pliers to close a crimp cover over the crimp.

[2] String 13 4mms and a repeating pattern of an 8mm accent bead and four 4mms four times.

[3] String two daisy spacers, an 8mm bicone crystal, two spacers, a 4mm, a beaded bead, and a 4mm. Repeat twice.

[4] String the second side as a mirror image of the first. Finish this end as in step 1.

[5] Open a 4mm jump ring (Basics), attach half of the clasp to one end of the necklace, and close the jump ring. Repeat on the other end.

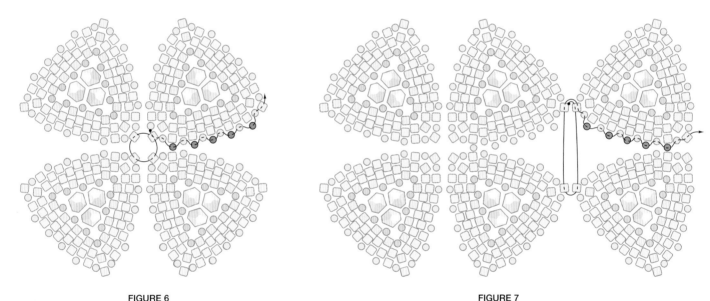

FIGURE 6

FIGURE 7

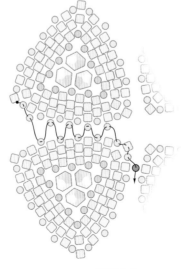

FIGURE 8

Royal
jewels

Re-create the look
of jewelry worn by
Russian tsarinas

designed by **Elizabeth Townes**

Elizabeth is fond of traditionally styled jewelry. Pairing hexagonal garnets with freshwater pearls creates the look of the jewel-encrusted necklaces and bracelets worn by Russian nobility of the 19th century. A gold-tone base completes the impression of regal riches.

step by step

Hexagonal base

[1] Center a needle on 3 yd. (2.7m) of thread, and pick up six 11º cylinder beads, leaving a 6-in. (15cm) tail. Sew through all the beads again to form a ring, and continue through the first cylinder picked up (**figure 1, a–b**). If you prefer to use Fireline, work with a single strand 1½ yd. (1.4m) in length.

[2] To form a disk, work in increasing circular peyote stitch (Peyote Basics, p. 5), stepping up through the first cylinder of each new round:

Round 2: Pick up one cylinder in each stitch (**b–c**).

Round 3: Pick up two cylinders in each stitch (**c–d**).

Round 4: Pick up one cylinder in each stitch, placing a cylinder between and in the middle of each pair (**d–e**).

Round 5: Pick up one cylinder in each stitch (**figure 2, a–b**).

Round 6: Alternate picking up one cylinder and picking up two cylinders in each stitch (**b–c**).

Round 7: Pick up one cylinder in each stitch, placing a cylinder after each cylinder in the previous round, including in the middle of each pair (**c–d**).

Round 8: Pick up one cylinder in each stitch (**figure 3, a–b**).

Round 9: Alternate working a stitch with two cylinders and working two stitches with one cylinder each (**b–c**).

Round 10: Pick up one cylinder in each stitch, placing a cylinder after each cylinder in the previous round, including in the middle of each pair (**c–d**).

[3] To add sides to the disk, work five rounds with one cylinder per stitch. Snug up the beads to form the sides (**photo a**). Do not end the working thread or tail.

[4] Repeat steps 1 and 2 to make a second disk. End the working thread and tail (Basics, p. 10).

[5] Zip up (Peyote Basics) the edges of the two parts, creating a hexagonal base (**photo b**). End the working thread and tail.

[6] Make three more hexagonal bases.

Base embellishments

Use a variety of beads to embellish the hexagonal bases. Sew through the base to attach the beads. Designer Elizabeth Townes created four embellishments combining fire-polished beads and round garnets; hexagonal garnets and seed pearls; bugle beads and seed beads; and round garnets, freshwater pearls, and garnet briolettes. Embellishment

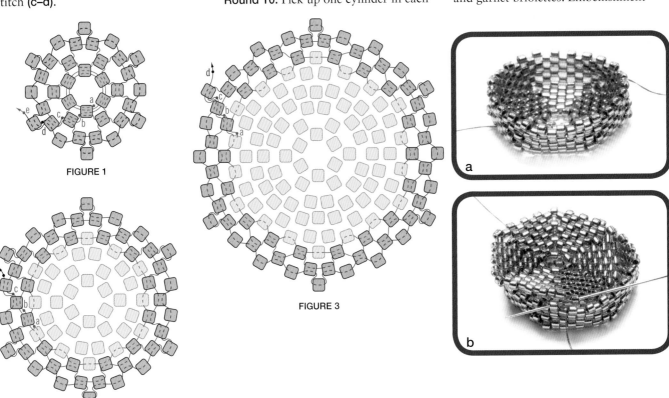

FIGURE 1

FIGURE 2

FIGURE 3

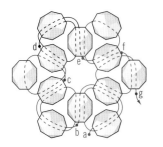

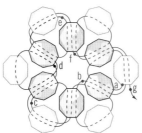

FIGURE 4

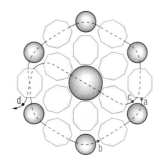

FIGURE 5

FIGURE 6

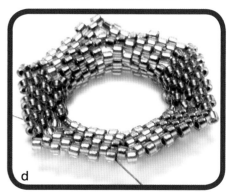

options include Czech teardrops and fire-polished beads, glass or round sterling silver beads, or gemstones. Following the examples shown on p. 79, place the beads in symmetrical patterns. Secure the larger beads first, and fill in around them.

Beaded spacers

[1] On 1 yd. (.9m) of thread or Fireline, pick up three 4 mm fire-polished beads, leaving a 6-in. (15cm) tail. Sew through all the beads again to form a ring (figure 4, a–b).

[2] Pick up two 4mms, and sew through the 4mm your thread exited and the two 4mms picked up in this step (b–c).

[3] Pick up two 4mms, and sew through the 4mm your thread exited and the first 4mm picked up in this step (c–d).

[4] Repeat steps 2 and 3 (d–e and e–f).

[5] Pick up one 4mm, and sew through the adjacent 4mm added in step 1, the last 4mm added in step 4, and the 4mm picked up in this step (f–g).

[6] To add the second side to the beaded spacer, pick up two 4mms, and sew through the edge 4mm your thread exited and the first 4mm picked up in this step (figure 5, a–b).

[7] Pick up one 4mm, and sew through the next edge 4mm, the first 4mm added in the previous step, the 4mm picked up in this step, and the next edge 4mm (b–c).

[8] Pick up one 4mm, and sew through the 4mm added in the previous step, the edge 4mm your thread exited, and the 4mm picked up in this step (c–d).

[9] Repeat steps 7 and 8 (d–e and e–f).

[10] Sew through the second 4mm added in step 6, the last edge 4mm, the 4mm added in the previous step, the 4mm added in step 6, and the next edge 4mm (f–g).

[11] Pick up a 2 or 3mm round bead and sew through the next edge 4mm (figure 6, a–b). Repeat to complete the round (b–c).

[12] Sew through an interior 4mm, pick up a 6mm bead, skip two interior 4mms, and sew through the next interior and edge 4mms (c–d).

[13] Flip the beadwork. Repeat step 12 on the other side. End the working thread and tail, and trim.

[14] Make two more beaded spacers.

Toggle loop

[1] On 3 yd. (2.7m) of thread or Fireline, pick up 36 cylinders, leaving a 6-in. (15cm) tail, and sew through the first cylinder again. Work three rows of tubular peyote (photo c).

[2] Work five rounds of increasing circular peyote, stepping up through the first cylinder of each new round:

Round 6: Alternate working two stitches with one cylinder each and one stitch with two cylinders.

Round 7: Pick up one cylinder in each stitch, placing a cylinder after each single cylinder and between each pair.

Round 8: Pick up one cylinder in each stitch.

Round 9: Pick up one cylinder in each stitch between the single stitches, and position a pair of cylinders to match the placement of the pairs of cylinders at the corners in round 6.

Round 10: Pick up one cylinder in each stitch, placing a cylinder after each single cylinder and between each pair (photo d).

[3] Sew through the beadwork to the opposite edge of the initial ring, exiting at a point where you can begin a repeat of round 6 in step 2, mirroring the stitching of the first side. Repeat step 2.

[4] Work three rounds of peyote with one cylinder per stitch. Snug up the beads to form the side edge of the toggle loop.

e

f

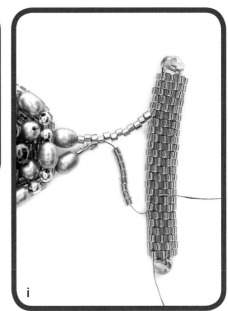

i

g

h

MATERIALS
bracelet 7¾ in. (19.7cm)
- **6** 6 x 5mm flat faceted briolettes
- **14** 6mm flat hexagonal beads
- **6** 6mm bugle beads
- **16** 5mm freshwater pearls, cross-drilled
- **7** 5mm freshwater pearls, drilled lengthwise
- **71** 4mm fire-polished beads
- **37** 2 or 3mm round beads
- **35** seed pearls
- **1g** 11º seed beads
- **15g** 11º cylinder beads
- nylon beading thread, size D, conditioned with beeswax or Thread Heaven, or Fireline, 6 lb. test
- beading needles, #12

[5] Zip up the two edges (photo e). End the working thread and tail.

Toggle bar
[1] On 2 yd. (1.8m) of thread or Fireline, attach a stop bead (Basics), leaving a 6-in. (15cm) tail. Working in flat even-count peyote (Peyote Basics), make a strip that is 24 beads wide with seven beads on each straight edge (14 rows). Remove the stop bead.
[2] Zip up the two edges, and sew through the beadwork to one end of the tube.
[3] Pick up a 4mm, and sew through the cylinder opposite the bead your thread exited at the start of this step.
[4] Sew through the beadwork to the other end of the tube, and repeat step 3. Sew through the beadwork, exiting six cylinders from the end of the tube. Do not end or trim the working thread or tail.

Assembly
[1] Using the working thread from the toggle bar, pick up 12 cylinders and a freshwater pearl.
[2] Sew through a hexagonal base, exiting the opposite side of the base (photo f).

[3] Pick up a freshwater pearl, and sew through an edge 4mm in a beaded spacer. Sew through the next six edge beads, exiting a 4mm (photo g). Pick up a freshwater pearl.
[4] Repeat steps 2 and 3 to attach the remaining hexagonal bases and beaded spacers.
[5] After attaching the last hexagonal base, pick up a freshwater pearl and 12 cylinders. Sew through a cylinder in a corner of the hexagonal toggle loop, and continue through the cylinders to the next corner. Pick up eight cylinders, sew through the ninth cylinder from the toggle loop, and pick up three cylinders and a freshwater pearl (photo h).
[6] Repeat steps 2 and 3 to sew back through the bracelet, adding a second pearl at each connection point between a hexagonal base and a beaded spacer.
[7] After sewing through the last hexagonal base, pick up a freshwater pearl and three cylinders. Sew through the fourth cylinder from the hexagonal base in the 12-cylinder section. Pick up eight cylinders, and sew through a cylinder six beads from the end of the toggle bar (photo i). End the working thread and tail, and trim.

Wildflower vine

Create realistic
petals using
sculptural peyote

designed by **Melissa Grakowsky**

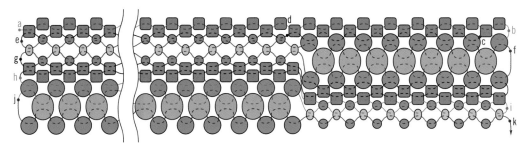

FIGURE 1

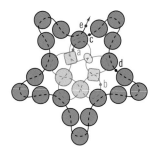

FIGURE 2

FIGURE 3

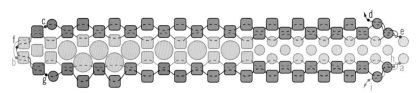

FIGURE 4

MATERIALS

necklace 14½ in. (36.8cm) with
flower centerpiece 2¼ in. (5.7cm)
diameter

- 8mm dentelle
- **5** 6mm bicone crystals
- **11** 4mm bicone crystals
- 2g 8º seed beads, color A
- 11º seed beads
  3g color A
  2g color B
  1g color C
- 11º cylinder beads
  7g color A
  2g each of **2** colors: B, C
  1g color D
- 15º seed beads
  2g color A
  3g each of **2** colors: B, C
  1g color D
- 1g 15º Charlottes, color A
- **3** 5mm bead caps, or **2** 5mm bead
  caps and a 5mm crystal disk bead
- Fireline, 6 lb. test
- beading needles, #12 or #13

Curling tendrils of vine and delicately shaped petals demonstrate the mastery of a fundamental stitch. Combine seed beads of different shapes, colors, and sizes for dramatic shaping that mimics nature.

stepbystep

Flower stem

[1] On 2 yd. (1.8m) of Fireline, pick up an even number of color A 11º cylinder beads until you have 7 in. (18cm) of beads, leaving a 12-in. (30cm) tail (figure 1, a–b).

[2] Turn, pick up a color A 11º seed bead, skip the last A cylinder, and sew through the next A cylinder (b–c). Work seven more peyote stitches (Peyote Basics, p. 5), picking up an A 11º in each stitch (c–d). Continue working in even-count peyote stitch to the end of the row, picking up a color A 15º seed bead per stitch (d–e).

[3] Continue working in even-count peyote stitch as follows, keeping your tension tight:

Row 4: Pick up a color A 15º Charlotte per stitch as you sew through the A 15ºs.

Pick up a color A 8º seed bead per stitch as you sew through the A 11ºs (e–f).

Row 5: Pick up an A 11º per stitch as you sew through the 8ºs. Pick up an A 15º as you sew through the Charlottes (f–g).

Rows 6 and 7: Pick up an A cylinder per stitch (g–h).

Row 8: Pick up an A 11º as you sew through the cylinders of the long segment. Pick up an A 15º as you sew through the cylinders of the short segment (h–i).

Row 9: Pick up an A Charlotte as you sew through the A 15ºs, and an A 8º as you sew through the A 11ºs (i–j).

Row 10: Pick up an A 11º as you sew through the 8ºs, and an A 15º as you sew through the Charlottes (j–k).

[4] Zip up (Peyote Basics) the edges of the tube, keeping the tension tight. You'll notice that the short section of the stem curves in one direction,

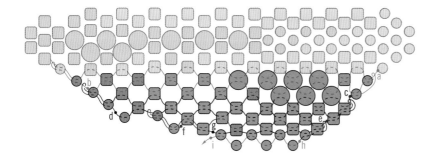

FIGURE 5

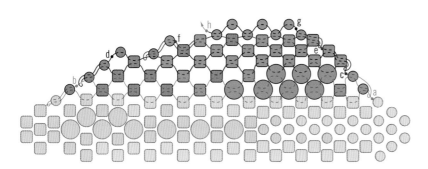

FIGURE 6

while the longer section spirals in the opposite direction.

[5] Exit an edge bead at one end. Pick up an A 11º, sew down through the next edge bead on the end, and up through the following bead **(figure 2, a–b)**. Repeat around the end to add five A 11ºs, and step up through the first A 11º added **(b–c)**.

[6] Pick up three A 11ºs, and sew through the next A 11º **(c–d)**. Repeat around the stem **(d–e)**. Do not end the thread.

[7] Using the tail, sew through the beadwork, and exit the other end of the stem. Pick up a bead cap and three A 11ºs, skip the 11ºs, and sew back through the bead cap and into the beadwork. Retrace the thread path several times to secure. Alternatively, pick up a 5mm crystal disk bead. Sew through the bead nearest to where your thread exited the disk. Retrace the thread path several times. End the tail (Basics, p. 10).

Petals

[1] Attach a needle to each end of a 1-yd. (.9m) length of Fireline. With one needle, pick up three color C cylinder beads, five color C 11º seed beads, a C cylinder, a C 11º, C cylinder, C 11º, C cylinder, C 11º, C cylinder, three color C 15º seed beads, and nine color B 15º seed beads **(figure 3, a–b)**, and pull them to the center of the thread.

[2] Using the other needle, work a row of peyote stitch as follows, picking up one bead per stitch: eight C cylinders, three C 15ºs, two B 15ºs. Pick up a B 15º **(d–e)**. Snug up the beads, and sew through the opposite end 15º with each needle **(b–c and e–f)**.

[3] With the lower needle, work a row of peyote stitch, picking up one bead per stitch, as follows: B 15º, seven B cylinder beads, C cylinder, B cylinder, three C cylinders **(figure 4, a–b)**.

[4] With the upper needle, work a row of peyote stitch as follows: B 15º, 10 B cylinders, two C cylinders **(e–f)**. Cross the needles through the two end beads, as in step 2, and step up to start the next rows **(b–c and f–g)**.

[5] With the lower needle, work a row of peyote stitch as follows: C 15º, C cylinder, two B cylinders, C cylinder, six

B cylinders, B 15º **(g–h)**. Sew under the thread bridge between the beads in the previous row, and back through the last two beads to make the turn and step up to start the next row **(h–i)**.

[6] With the upper needle, work a row of peyote stitch as follows: C 15º, C cylinder, nine B cylinders, B 15º. Turn, and step up as in step 5 **(c–d)**.

[7] With the lower needle, work the remaining rows in peyote as follows, making the turn as in step 5 at the end of each row:

Row 1: B 15º, B cylinder, four color B 11º seed beads, two B cylinders, two C cylinders, C 15º **(figure 5, a–b)**.

Row 2: C 15º, C cylinder, three B cylinders, C cylinder, three B 11ºs, B 15º **(b–c)**.

Row 3: Seven B cylinders, C cylinder, C 15º **(c–d)**.

Row 4: Two C 15ºs, six B cylinders **(d–e)**.

Row 5: Three B cylinders, C cylinder, B cylinder, B 15º **(e–f)**. Note that this row stops one stitch short of the end of the row.

Row 6: Sew through the next two beads to skip a stitch and step up to start the next row **(f–g)**. Four B 15ºs **(g–h)**.

Row 7: Three B 15ºs **(h–i)**. Do not end the thread.

[8] With the upper needle, complete the remaining rows in peyote stitch as follows, making the turn as in step 5:

Row 1: B 15º, B cylinder, four B 11ºs, B cylinder, three C cylinders, C 15º **(figure 6, a–b)**.

Row 2: C 15º, two C cylinders, B cylinder, C cylinder, B cylinder, three B 11ºs, B 15º **(b–c)**.

Row 3: Seven B cylinders, C cylinder, C 15º **(c–d)**.

Row 4: Two C 15ºs, C cylinder, five B cylinders **(d–e)**.

Row 5: Three B cylinders, C cylinder, B cylinder, B 15º **(e–f)**. Note that this is a short row.

Row 6: Sew through the next two beads to skip a stitch and step up. Stitch four B 15ºs **(f–g)**.

Row 7: Three B 15ºs **(g–h)**. Do not end the thread.

[9] Repeat steps 1–8 to make four more petals.

FIGURE 7

FIGURE 8

FIGURE 9

Center

[1] On 1 yd. (.9m) of Fireline, center 22 color D cylinder beads, and sew through the first D cylinder again (**figure 7, a–b**).

[2] Work a round of tubular peyote stitch (Basics), picking up a D cylinder for each stitch (**b–c**). Work two rounds of tubular peyote, picking up a color D 15º seed bead for each stitch (**c–d**).

[3] Place the 8mm dentelle face up in the bezel, and, using the tail, work two rounds of tubular peyote using D 15ºs to complete the bezel and secure the dentelle.

[4] Sew through the beadwork to exit a D cylinder in the uppermost round. Pick up a 4mm bicone crystal and a D 15º, and sew back through the 4mm. Continue through the next D cylinder in the round (**figure 8**). Repeat around, and step up to exit a D 15º in the top round.

[5] Pick up five D 15ºs, a 6mm bicone crystal, and a D 15º. Sew back through the 6mm and the next five 15ºs. Continue through the next 15º in the round, the next 15º in the previous round, and the next 15º (**figure 9**). Repeat around to add four more 6mms. The spacing will not be quite even.

Assembly

[1] With one of the tails from a petal, sew down through the edge beads to exit the next edge cylinder. Pick up a B cylinder, and sew through the next edge B 15º on the petal (**figure 10, a–b**). Sew through the next edge bead, a C 15º. Pick up a C 15º, and sew through the next C 15º (**b–c**). Pull the beads snug.

[2] Using the tail from a second petal, repeat step 1, sewing through the beads just added to the adjacent petal (**e–f**).

[3] Use one thread to sew the remaining edge beads together following a square stitch (Basics) thread path (**c–d**). Once the join is secure, end both threads.

[4] Repeat steps 1–3 to join two more petals to the first pair.

[5] Using the tails from the center of the flower, stitch between the color D beads surrounding the dentelle and the color C cylinders at the base of the joined petals. There is no set thread path, just sew between the beads, keeping the thread hidden as much as possible.

[6] Repeat steps 1–3 to attach the remaining petal to the flower. Secure the dentelle to the final petal, and end all the working threads and tails.

[7] To secure the stem to the flower, match the five points of the end of the stem to the five petals of the flower. Using a modified square stitch (Basics) thread path, sew back and forth between the petals and the stem until the flower is secure. End the threads.

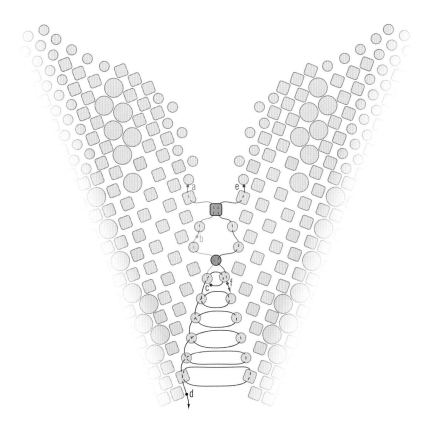

FIGURE 10

EDITOR'S NOTE:
If stiff tension in your necklace makes it difficult to join five petals in a circle, try adding a sixth petal. The resulting flower will be more open, so you may choose to omit the 6mm bicones from the center of the flower.

Necklace

[1] On 2 yd. (1.8m) of Fireline, pick up an even number of A cylinders to equal the desired length of the necklace, less ½ in. (1.3cm) to allow for the end curves. Turn, and work eight rows of even-count peyote stitch, for a total of 10 rows. Zip up the edges of the strip to form a long tube.

[2] On 30 in. (76cm) of Fireline, pick up 32 A cylinders. Turn, and work eight rows of even-count peyote as follows:
Row 3: One A 15º per stitch.
Row 4: One A Charlotte per stitch.
Row 5: One A 15º per stitch.
Rows 6 and 7: One A cylinder per stitch.
Row 8: One A 11º per stitch.
Row 9: One A 8º per stitch.
Row 10: One A 11º per stitch.

[3] Zip up the edges to form a tight, curved tube. Exiting a bead at the end of the tube, sew under the thread bridge between two beads at one end of the tube made in step 1. Sew back through the bead your thread exited. Repeat around the tubes to join the curved segment to the cylinder segment.

[4] Sew through the beadwork to exit the other end of the curved segment. Pick up a bead cap and three A 11ºs, skip the 11ºs, and sew back through the bead cap and into the beadwork. Retrace the thread path several times to secure.

[5] Repeat steps 2–4 to finish the other end of the necklace.

[6] Wind the flower stem around the necklace, and loop the curved ends around each other to clasp.

The curling tendrils of the stem act as the pendant bail and the clasp for this lovely necklace.

Interlocking links

Weave peyote stitch links into a seamless cuff

designed by **Jacqueline Johnson**

The bicolored links in this bracelet give the impression of complex woven layers — by looking at the completed piece, you can't tell that the links are actually two colors. And if you don't know the secret, the illusion that these multiple rows of links have no beginning or end will keep you guessing to infinity and beyond!

stepbystep

Links

[1] On 5 ft. (1.5m) of conditioned thread (Basics, p. 10), pick up four color A 13º Charlottes. Sew through the first bead again to form a ring.

[2] Continue using A 13ºs and work in tubular, even-count peyote (Peyote Basics, p. 5) for a total of eight rounds. Keep your tension consistent, but not too tight, so the links are soft and bendable.

MATERIALS
bracelet 7½ in. (19.1cm)
- 15g 13º Charlottes, in each of **2** colors: A, C
- 15g 15º Japanese seed beads, in each of **2** colors: B, D
- nylon beading thread, size B or D, conditioned with beeswax
- beading needles, #13

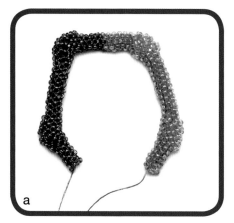

a

b

c

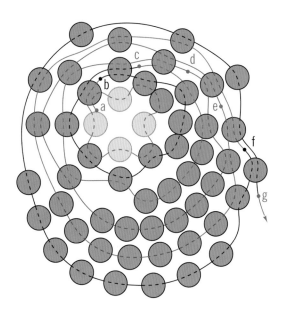

FIGURE 1

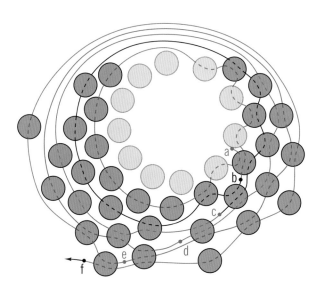

FIGURE 2

[3] To form the first corner of the link, use A 13ºs, and alter the number of beads picked up in the second stitch of rounds 9–18 as follows. Sew through the first bead of each round to step up and through the first bead of the second stitch as you work each round.

Round 9: A, two As, A, A **(figure 1, a–b)**
Round 10: A, three As, A, A **(b–c)**
Round 11: A, five As, A, A **(c–d)**
Round 12: A, seven As, A, A **(d–e)**
Round 13: A, eight As, A, A **(e–f)**
Round 14: A, eight As, A, A **(f–g)**
Round 15: A, seven As, A, A **(figure 2, a–b)**
Round 16: A, five As, A, A **(b–c)**
Round 17: A, three As, A, A **(c–d)**
Round 18: A, two As, A, A **(d–e)**

[4] Continue working four beads per round in tubular, even-count peyote (e–f) for 19 rounds.

[5] Repeat step 3 to make the second corner.

[6] Work eight rounds in tubular, even-count peyote to complete the first half of the link.

[7] Repeat steps 2–6 using color B 15º seed beads **(photo a)**. Don't secure or cut the threads.

[8] Make a total of 18 links, nine in color A 13ºs and color B 15ºs, and nine in color C 13ºs and color D 15ºs.

Assembly

[1] Align the first and last rows of a color AB link, and zip up (Peyote Basics and **photo b**) the two ends to complete the link. End the threads (Basics).

[2] Twist the AB link so the 13º half of the link crosses over the top of the 15ºs, forming a figure 8 **(photo c)**.

[3] Position a CD link as shown in **photo d** so the 15º half of the CD link is looped through the bottom ring of the AB link.

[4] Form a figure 8 with the CD link so the 13º half of the link loops through the top ring of the AB link **(photo e)**.

[5] Align the first and last rows of the CD link, and stitch the two ends together as you did in step 1. End the threads **(photo f)**.

[6] Repeat steps 3–5 with an AB link **(photo g)**.

[7] Continue connecting the links, alternating between AB and CD links. Join the 18th link to the 17th and to the first link to complete the cuff.

d

e

f

EDITOR'S NOTE:
As you make the links, count out the beads needed for each round listed in a step and line them up on your work surface. This will help you keep track of what round you are on, and when you run out of beads for the row, it will remind you to step up.

g

Decorative *vessels*

Dress up peyote stitch containers with lively embellished lids

designed by **Wendy Ellsworth**

Colorful beaded baskets work up rather quickly using 8º Japanese seed beads and two-, three-, and four-drop peyote. You'll be surprised to see how soon you have a cute little container for storing — what else? — more beads!

stepbystep

If you are using nylon beading thread, use it doubled and with moderate tension. It isn't necessary to double Fireline. Wendy used 3-yd. (2.7m) lengths and added thread four times to complete the container.

Container base
[1] On 3 yd. (2.7m) of Fireline or doubled thread, pick up three color A 8º seed beads, and tie them into a ring with a square knot (Basics, p. 10), leaving a 6-in. (15cm) tail. Sew through the next bead (**figure 1, a–b**).
[2] Work in flat, circular peyote (Peyote Basics, p. 5) as follows:

Round 2: Increase by picking up two color B 8ºs per stitch. Step up through the first two Bs added in this step (**b–c**).
Round 3: Six As, adding a bead between each pair of beads from round 2 (**c–d**).
Round 4: Two Bs per stitch (**d–e**).
Round 5: One A per stitch, as in round 3 (**e–f**).
Round 6: One B per stitch (**f–g**).
Round 7: Alternate between two As and one A per stitch (**g–h**).
Round 8: One B per stitch, sewing through both increase beads from the previous round (**h–i**).
Round 9: Two As per stitch (**i–j**).
Round 10: Alternate between

one B and two Bs per stitch (**j–k**).
Round 11: Two As per stitch (**k–l**).
Round 12: Two Bs per stitch (**l–m**).
Round 13: Alternate between two As and three As per stitch (**m–n**). This is the last row of the bottom of the vessel. (The bottom may not lie flat, but this can be addressed later.)

Walls
Work in two-, three-, and four-drop circular peyote as follows, monitoring your tension for each row by not letting the thread show. End and add thread (Basics) as needed.
Round 14: Two Bs per stitch.
Round 15: Three As per stitch.

MATERIALS
container with lid
- assortment of 4–8mm accent beads for cover
- **45** 4mm fringe beads
- 45g 8º Japanese seed beads, in each of **2** colors: A, B
- nylon beading thread, size D, conditioned with beeswax; Power Pro; or Fireline 10 lb. test
- beading needles, #10

Round 16–23: Repeat rounds 14 and 15 four times.
Round 24: Alternate between two Bs and three Bs per stitch.
Round 25: Three As per stitch.
Round 26: Three Bs per stitch.
Round 27–28: Repeat rounds 25 and 26.

Use a variety of glass and natural beads to add a burst of contrasting color to your containers.

Round 29: Alternate between three As and four As per stitch.
Round 30: Three Bs per stitch.
Round 31: Four As per stitch.
Round 32–35: Repeat rounds 30 and 31 twice.
Round 36: Alternate between three Bs and four Bs per stitch.
Round 37: Four As per stitch.
Round 38: Four Bs per stitch.
Round 39–50: Repeat rounds 37 and 38 six times.
Round 51: Four As per stitch.
Round 52: Three Bs per stitch.
Round 53: Four As per stitch.
Round 54–65: Alternate between rounds of three Bs per stitch and three As per stitch six times. End the threads.

Lid

[1] Start a new thread, and pick up an alternating pattern of three As and three Bs 13 times. Tie the beads into a ring, and place them around the top rim of the container (photo a).
[2] Working in three-drop peyote, complete 10 rounds, ending with As. Work these rounds on the container so the lid is the correct size. Adjust your tension as you work so the lid isn't too tight (photo b). Continue working in circular peyote. Begin with two- and three-drop, then decrease to single peyote as follows:
Round 11: Two Bs per stitch.
Round 12: Three As per stitch.
Round 13: Two Bs per stitch.
Round 14: Two As per stitch.
Round 15: Two Bs per stitch.
Round 16: One A per stitch.
Round 17–26: Repeat rounds 15 and 16 five times.
Round 27: One B per stitch.
Round 28: One A per stitch.
Round 29: Decrease to 10 beads in this round: Stitch the next four Bs, one bead per stitch (figure 2, a–b). Then skip a stitch by sewing through the next A (b–c). Work three Bs (one bead per stitch), skip a stitch, and work three Bs as before. Skip the last stitch, and step up through the first B added in this step (c–d).
Round 30: Decrease to nine beads in this round: Stitch one A, skip a stitch, then work the remaining stitches with As (d–e).
Round 31: Decrease to three beads in this round: Stitch one B every third stitch (e–f).
Round 32: One A per stitch (f–g). Reinforce the last round with a second thread path.

Embellishment

[1] Add a new thread, and pick up enough accent beads to fit around the ledge of the lid (photo c). Sew the beads into a ring, and secure the tails. If the ring is very loose, sew through a few beads on the lid to secure it.
[2] Exit the last round of the lid, and pick up one or two fringe beads (photo d), depending on how much space is between the beads. Sew through the next bead in the last round. Continue to add as many fringe beads as desired. End the threads. Push gently on the bottom to curve it inward (photo e).

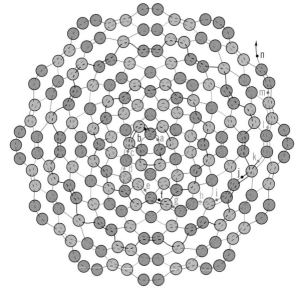

FIGURE 1

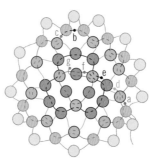

FIGURE 2

a

b

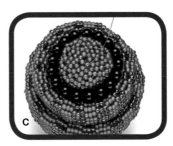

c

d

e

EDITOR'S NOTE:
Check the seed beads for irregularities. While these "imperfect" beads are usually discarded, in a project like this, an irregular bead may be just the right size to fill in a stitch perfectly.

Contributors

Kathryn Bowman is a lifelong artist now working with beads and metal. Always sharing her jewelry skills, Kathryn has cultivated an active teaching and writing life. Contact Kathryn via e-mail at 1kathrynbowman@gmail.com, or visit her website, 1beadweaver.com.

Antonio Calles began beading many years ago after trying several different crafts. He now teaches others how to bead, and continues to create a variety of original pieces of jewelry using many different stitches. Contact Antonio in care of Kalmbach Books.

Jennifer Creasey began beading in 1991 and especially enjoys designing patterns with Alaskan and Native American themes. When she's not beading, she crochets or cross-stitches. Visit Jennifer's website, polarbeads.com.

Anna Elizabeth Draeger is an associate editor at *Bead&Button* magazine and author of *Crystal Brilliance*. Contact her via e-mail at adraeger@ beadandbutton.com, or visit her website, web.mac.com/beadbiz.

Rev. Wendy Ellsworth is a full-time studio seed bead artist living in Bucks County, Pa. Visit her website at ellsworthstudios.com.

Linda Gettings enjoys working on intricate designs in both beadweaving and wirework. She is a full-time jewelery designer, teacher, and writer. Contact her via e-mail at ladybeading@aol.com.

Julie Glasser is a beadweaving artist who has been teaching off-loom stitching since 2002. Visit her website, julieglasser.com.

Beading is a natural fit for **Melissa Grakowsky**, who has a background in physics and painting and enjoys the problem-solving aspects and three-dimensional possibilities of beading. Contact Melissa via e-mail at grakowsky@ gmail.com, or visit her website, grakowsky.net.

Jonna Holston lives in Kernersville, N.C. She teaches her designs in weekly beading classes. Contact Jonna at gianabijou@yahoo.com.

Full-time bead artist **Pamm Horbit** lives in the Northwest and enjoys working with three-dimensional geometric designs. Contact her through her website, whitelotusbeading.com.

After 30 years of working in graphic design, **Virginia Jensen** finds it natural to apply design principles to beading techniques. Virgina is the author of *Cube Bead Stitching* and *Cube Bead Stitching 2*. Visit her website, virjenmettle.com.

Contact **Jacqueline Johnson** via e-mail at jackie@jjattic.com, or visit her website, jjattic.com.

Contact **Barbara Klann** in care of Kalmbach Books.

Cathy Lampole of Ontario, Canada, enjoys the fine detail that can be achieved with beadweaving. Besides designing jewelry, Cathy owns a bead shop, That Bead Lady. Contact her at cathy@ thatbeadlady.com.

Laura McCabe has been beading for a lifetime and enjoys using unconventional materials. Visit her website, justletmebead.com, or contact her via e-mail at justletmebead@gmail.com.

Marina Nadke lives in Dortmund, Germany. During a trip to Canada, she saw her first beading magazine and fell in love with the craft. She now teaches classes and creates one-of-a-kind jewelry pieces. Her favorite projects take time to make, and she says that designing new projects is "like dreaming with open eyes." Visit her website at marina-original.de, or contact her by e-mail at marina.nadke@t-online.de.

Cindy Thomas Pankopf teaches beading in Southern California and at the Bead&Button Show, and is also a senior instructor for Art Clay Silver. She is the author of *BeadMaille* and *The Absolute Beginners Guide: Making Metal Clay Jewelry*. Contact her via e-mail at info@cindypankopf.com, or visit her website, cindypankopf.com.

Contact **Rebecca Peapples** via e-mail at rspeapples@aol.com.

Elaine Pinckney lives in Dacula, Ga. Contact her via e-mail at ebeadchaser@ bellsouth.net.

Jean Power is an award-winning designer who loves to play with shape and color. Contact her via e-mail at jean@jeanpower.com, or visit her website, jeanpower.com.

Karmen Schmidt is a devoted beader who creates original beadwork using many techniques and media. Contact her via e-mail at schmidt1@ccwebster.net.

The late **Gillian "Gill" Slone** was a beader for more than 12 years, had more than 20 projects published in magazines and books, and created finished jewelry on commission and for sale to the public. Gill lived in Wharfedale, North Yorkshire, England.

Beth Stone is truly passionate about beads and has a creative style and original approach to seed bead stitching that are unique in the beading world. Beth is the author of *Seed Bead Stitching*, *More Seed Bead Stitching*, and *Bead, Play, & Love*. Contact her via e-mail at bnshdl@msn.com, or visit her website, bethstone.com.

Jewelry designer **Elizabeth Townes** lives in Tampa, Fla. She enjoys silversmithing and making lampwork beads, as well as creating beadwoven designs. Contact her via e-mail at info@beadjeweledinc.com, or visit her website, beadjeweledinc.com.

Angie Weathers lives in Pooler, Ga., and has been beading since 2001. Contact her via e-mail at wowmaw@aol.com, or visit her website, wowmawbeads.blogspot.com.

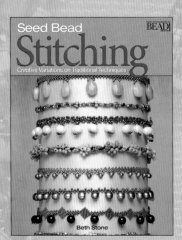